THE IMPACT OF IMMIGRATION ON THE UNITED STATES ECONOMY

Augustine J. Kposowa

University Press of America,® Inc.
Lanham • New York • Oxford

Copyright © 1998
University Press of America,® Inc.
4720 Boston Way
Lanham, Maryland 20706

12 Hid's Copse Rd.
Cummor Hill, Oxford OX2 9JJ

Library of Congress Cataloging-in-Publication Data

Kposowa, Augustine J.
The impact of immigration on the United States economy /
Augustine J. Kposowa.
p.   cm.
Includes bibliographical references and index.
1. United States—Emigration and immigration—Economic
aspects—economic aspects. 2. Manpower policy—United States.
I. Title.
JV6471.K66 1998 330.973—dc21   98-14290 CIP

ISBN 0-7618-1092-7 (cloth: alk. ppr.)
ISBN 0-7618-1093-5 (pbk: alk. ppr.)

Preface

In recent years, the question of immigration (both legal and illegal) has become a truly controversial and highly politicized issue in the United States. The passage of Proposition 187 in California and recent bills in the U.S. congress that sought to deny public education to children of undocumented immigrants and eliminate various forms of public assistance to legal immigrants are just minor indications of a broader public attitude to the perceived consequences of immigration on American society.

Immigrants have been blamed for everything, including unemployment among native born citizens, earnings and wage depression, crime, 'terrorism', public dependence, and cultural change. The latter is presumably brought about by some immigrants insisting on speaking their own language, and failing to, or refusing to assimilate into 'mainstream' Anglo-American culture.

While native born Americans have not always welcomed all immigrant groups with equal enthusiasm, the present uneasiness toward newcomers appears unprecedented. Indeed, the very term used to describe immigrants with immutable persistence in government documents and public discourse--*aliens*— conjures up images of uninvited beings landing on the United States from strange planets and galaxies, seemingly poised to initiate an imminent invasion.

At an even deeper political level, there are some who believe that in addition to affecting the U.S. economy negatively, immigrants are responsible for perceived increases in various forms of criminality. From the near devastation of the World Trade Center complex in New York City, the bombing of the Murray Federal building in Oklahoma City, initial public and official reactions to the fatal TWA Flight 800 crash off Long Island, to the explosion of an incendiary device at the 1996 Olympic Games in Atlanta, and the uncovering of an alleged 1997 plot by certain individuals or groups to engage in hostile action against U.S. domestic targets, policy makers and politicians have concluded that 'terrorism' in America is the work of immigrants.

Accordingly, American politicians have adopted a sort of knee-jerk reaction (more and immediate legislation) to deal with social and economic problems, including immigration reform. The 1996 "Antiterrorism and Effective Death Penalty Act", for example, appears more targeted at immigrants and immigration than combating terrorism, and implicitly limits immigrants from protection under the Bill of Rights. It removes the rights of immigrants to challenge deportation, even if they have no idea why they are being deported. As a consequence, for the first time in over two hundred years of American history, secret information may be entered as evidence in court and go unchallenged. The antiterrorism act has effectively destroyed the Writ of Habeas Corpus, even as the President and other government officials continue to maintain that the bill is not tough enough. It may well be that in the waning years of the 20th century, and well into the 21st, the standard of election or reelection for prosecutors, judges and politicians may not be "tough on crime", but instead "tough on immigration".

The issues surrounding immigration are truly complex. What this book does is not so much to cover every conceivable aspect of immigration, but to provide objective and empirical evidence regarding the effects of immigration on the U.S. with emphasis on (1) native earnings, (2) industries, (3) social mobility of natives, (4) unemployment, (5) public assistance dependence, and (6) Social Security reception. Other issues, for example, the link between crime, proscribed drugs, 'terrorism' and immigration are the focus of another book now in the making.

Three chapters draw on materials that have been published previously. An earlier version of chapter 6 was published in Augustine J. Kposowa, "The Impact of Immigration on Native Earnings", *Applied Behavioral Science Review* (1993) 1:1-25, and Augustine J. Kposowa, "The Impact of Immigration on Unemployment and Earnings Among Racial Minorities in the United States", *Ethnic and Racial Studies* (1995) 606-628. Chapter 10 is based on Augustine J. Kposowa "Immigration and Economic Dependence in the U.S.", *Applied Behavioral Science Review* (1995) 3:65-83.

A. J. K.

iv

Contents

ix

Chapter 1

Introduction

The study of immigration and its relationship to the labor market has a long tradition in the United States, dating back to the late 19th century (Abbott, 1926; Bernard, 1953, 1965; Hutchinson, 1956; Rayback, 1966; Lebergott, 1964). Recent discussions, especially in the last two decades have focused on two main questions: (1) What do immigrants bring to the U.S. labor market? (2) What do immigrants do to the American labor market? Research dealing with the first question has concentrated on the human capital and other characteristics of immigrants, especially in relation to natives. The second question concerns the impact that immigrants have on U.S. workers.

In the late 1970's and early 1980's, in particular, as public concern over the poor performance of the U.S. economy grew, the perception that immigrants made a substantial contribution to the nation's economic woes became widespread. That perception was especially fueled by highly publicized and often sensationalistic media coverage of the volume of illegal immigration.

Although immigration is currently not the largest component of population growth in the United States (Borjas and Tienda, 1987:645) and despite evidence that earlier historical periods witnessed much larger inflows (Fallow, 1985:8; U.S. Department of Justice 1993:27-28; Borjas, 1994) there are some who believe that unless present levels are reduced, immigration could have detrimental effects on American society. Lamm and Imhoff, for example (1985:76-77) asserted that:

> Massive immigration involves serious and profound social and cultural dangers. The United States is not immune to the threats that have affected and altered all other human societies. Civilizations rise and civilizations fall —and there are certain universal pathologies that characterize the fall of history's civilizations—ethnic, racial, and religious differences can become such a pathology; they can grow faster, and eventually splinter a society...America's culture and national identity are threatened by massive levels of legal and illegal immigration.

Along similar lines, Fauriol (1985:96) argued that:

> the security of the United States has suffered in the past as a result of the government's impotency in the face of massive illegal immigration, and it will continue to suffer as the situation increasingly worsens. Employment levels, domestic political cohesion, national resources and the global standing of the United States can all be adversely affected by the current state of U.S. immigration policy.

The foregoing arguments are not new in the immigration debate. Immigration opponents and restrictionists argued in the second quarter of the 19th century that new immigrants comprised an unusually high percentage of criminals, that they placed excessive demands on charitable institutions, and that in general, they damaged American standards of living (Taylor, 1971:239).

Among the ongoing controversies surrounding continued immigration is the perception that immigrants, notably recent ones, have negative effects on the U.S. labor market in terms of wage and employment levels of the native born. Johnson (1980:331) affirmed that:

> Immigrants compete directly with the domestic population in the labor market. Whether this results in increased unemployment, lower wages, or a

reduction in the labor-force participation of the
domestic low-skilled population, the latter will in
the short run be worse off due to additional
immigration.

Briggs (1984b:ii) argued that "immigrants participate in the labor
force and consume public services which are partially financed by tax
payers." Others have pointed out that skill levels of immigrants have
deteriorated since 1968, and that should current trends continue, the U.S.
labor market will be adversely affected (Matta and Popp, 1988).
Chiswick (1986:168-192) reported that the earnings of immigrant adult
males from countries other than Britain have fallen since 1965 relative
to the earnings of immigrants from Britain. He also noted that
educational levels of immigrant males from countries other than Europe
and Canada have decreased or remained unchanged.

The last two decades have seen dramatic changes in the volume
and composition of immigrants to the United States (Bean, Telles and
Lowell, 1987:671; Bean and Sullivan, 1985; Massey, 1981; Briggs,
1984a). Not only has the number of immigrants increased, but their
national origins have shifted from Europe to less developed countries,
mainly in Asia and Latin America. Between 1951 and 1960, Europeans
comprised 53 percent of all immigrants. However, during the 1970s, they
made up less than 20 percent of new immigrants. At the same time,
persons from Asia and Latin America increased their representation in
immigrants admitted from 6 and 40 percent respectively in the 1950s to
35 and 44 percent during the 1970s. In the 1980s, Asians were 37.3
percent of all legal immigrants, while the percentage of entrants from the
Americas was 49.3. In the same period, Europeans made up only 10.4
percent of new (legal) immigrants (U.S. Department of Justice, 1986:3-5;
1993:27-28).

As the volume and composition of recent immigrant streams have
changed, the attention of the public and policy makers has focused on the
liabilities rather than the assets associated with the new immigrants.
Current public concerns about immigration center around a number of
fears about the labor market and other societal effects (Cafferty,
Chiswick, Greeley and Sullivan, 1983; Borjas and Tienda, 1987). The
first fear is that the number of immigrants has increased beyond a level
that can be absorbed by the American labor market. The second is that
new immigrants displace native workers by taking jobs away from them.

This presumably leads to increases in native unemployment levels. Third, immigrants are viewed as lowering American wages. Fourth, since the sources of new immigrants have changed, the new immigration could lead to dramatic changes in the racial and ethnic composition of the American population and labor force. It is estimated, for example, that over 80 percent of immigrants and refugees admitted to the United States since the 1970s have come from Latin America and Asia (Bean, Vernez, and Keely, 1989; Briggs, 1987:179;). Relatedly, new immigrants are seen as being less assimilable into American culture in comparison with earlier arrivals. Consequently, continuous immigration from developing countries could in the long run break the social cohesion of American society, especially in terms of language, culture, and politics (Fuchs, 1984:800-813). Finally, it has often been assumed that immigrants use transfer income, and they therefore, depend upon U.S. tax revenues and social services for sustenance (Johnson, 1980; Marshall, 1984; Tienda, Jensen and Bach, 1984; Borjas and Trejo, 1991). Recently, some analysts have revived interest in immigrant criminality, ranging from illicit drug trafficking to U.S. domestic 'terrorism' (Murphy, 1994; Lutton and Tanton, 1994; Tanton and Lutton, 1993).

Empirical findings about the above fears and other possible negative impacts of immigrants on U.S. society have not been conclusive or consistent. While some researchers have for example, reported that immigration has harmful effects on the U.S. labor market (Briggs, 1984a; Borjas, 1994), others have provided contrary evidence (Borjas and Tienda, 1987; Bean, Telles, and Lowell, 1987; Freeman, 1988; Simon, Moore, and Sullivan, 1993). Borjas and Tienda (1987:647) for example, pointed out that:

> On the one hand, foreign and native workers may be substitutes in the production process in that they perform the same types of jobs and have the same kinds of skills. Under these circumstances, an increase in the supply of immigrants will lower the native wage rate (and level of employment). On the other hand, foreign and native workers may be complements in production ... As the supply of immigrants rises, native workers can gain by specializing in those industries and occupations in which they have a comparative advantage.

Much has been written on immigration, both legal and illegal. However, there are some limitations in previous studies. First, investigators have primarily used cross-sectional designs. While reliance on cross-sectional data offers insights into labor market effects of more recent immigrants, it fails to illustrate whether findings reflect just period-specific effects or long-term cohort effects. Thus, more dynamic aspects of the labor market consequences of immigration are missed. While it is important to know the effects of immigration on society for a given time period, from a policy point of view, it is equally or even more important to know whether such effects persist or disappear with time.

Second, past researchers have limited their investigations of the labor market impacts of immigration to determinants of earnings. Although earnings represent a good measure of labor market outcomes gained by individuals or groups, it is not the only benefit. Previous studies have ignored such important variables as socioeconomic status, occupational prestige, and the industrial sectors in which native born workers are employed as a consequence of immigration. Finally, many studies lack strong theoretical perspectives to provide their hypotheses or guide their arguments. Findings are usually presented from mainly (ad hoc) economic oriented points of view.

The present research departs from previous works and aims at advancing our understanding of the labor market effects of immigration in three general aspects: First, it uses a trend (longitudinal) design. The period covered by the analysis, 1940 to 1980, was a dynamic and rather interesting epoch in American history. Many economic, political, social, and legal conditions changed remarkably during this period. On the economic front, the prosperity of the 1950s and 1960s gave way to increases in unemployment, inflation rates, and recessions in the 1970s and early 1980s. In the political realm, America moved away from its pre-Second World War isolationist foreign policy, and became a major economic and military power with assumed global responsibilities. The country also participated in the Second World War, a war in Korea, and a war in Vietnam. On the social level, various mass movements changed the nation forever. These included the civil rights movement, the women's movement, student protests, and the anti-war movement. The legal realm saw a notable change in U.S. immigration policy in 1965, and this policy shift may have affected immigration well into the 1980s and 1990s. A trend design in this book helps us understand how some of these changes influenced immigration to the United States, and how the former affected the labor market.

Second, apart from earnings, this study focuses on socioeconomic attainment, unemployment, and industrial sector as major indicators of labor market outcomes. Such a focus provides a more comprehensive and sociologically grounded approach to understanding and explaining the impact of immigration on the labor market and U.S. born workers. Finally, this book derives hypotheses from human capital theory, dual labor market theory, and equilibrium theory. It uses the three perspectives to explain the mechanisms by which immigration affects the labor market. Ultimately, findings observed are explained within the framework of the three theories.

The aim of the project to be undertaken is to examine the effects of immigration on the U.S. labor market, and to determine whether or not immigration has benefitted or hurt the United States. Due to data limitations, the study does not distinguish between types of immigrants. Distinctions are not made between legal and illegal immigrants, or refugees. The focus is on immigrants as a group. The specific problems being clarified are the following:

1. Do immigrants depress American earnings?
2. Do immigrants lower American socioeconomic attainment or occupational prestige?
3. Are immigrants in secondary labor markets, and if so, are there any negative repercussions on the native born?
4. Do immigrants affect the industrial sector in which Americans are present?
5. Do immigrants displace American workers, and if so what is the extent of the impact of immigration on native minorities?
6. Do immigrants use public assistance, and if so, are they more likely than native born Americans to depend on public assistance?
7. To what extent do all of the answers to the above problems conform to, or deviate from findings of previous immigration research?
8. What are the implications of answers to the above problems for current and future U.S. immigration policy?

Organization of the Book

Chapter 2 presents the theoretical frameworks guiding the study. These are human capital, dual labor market, and equilibrium theories. Various hypotheses on the labor market effects of immigration are also derived from these theories.

In Chapter 3, past studies are reviewed as are considered relevant to the present research. The review first undertakes a brief survey of U.S. immigration history, and then presents previous research evidence on various aspects of the U.S. labor market. These include: the geographic distribution of immigrants, changes in the countries of origin of immigrants, and the effects of immigration on the U.S. labor market in terms of earnings depression and displacement. Chapter 3 closes with discussions on the extent of immigrant dependence on public assistance.

Sources of data, definitions of variables, and statistical methods are outlined in Chapter 4. Chapter 5 begins the analysis section with a summary of the descriptive statistics. The next chapter (6) gives findings on the effects of immigration on earnings at both individual and aggregate levels of analysis. The first section gives results on individual determinants of earnings, and the second section presents findings on the impact of immigrants on American earnings. Chapter 7 gives similar analysis on the effects of immigration on American socioeconomic attainment and occupational prestige.

Dual labor market theorists hold that immigrants tend to be located in secondary labor markets. Findings on the industrial sector in which immigrants are present are discussed in chapter 8. Additionally, the extent to which immigrants affect the sectors in which Americans are employed is also discussed in the same chapter.

Some past studies have found that immigrants displace American workers by driving them into unemployment. Results on the displacing effects of immigration on the native born are discussed in chapter 9.

A frequently raised, but relatively under researched topic is the perception that immigrants tend to depend on public assistance financed by American taxpayers. Analysis of the extent to which the foregoing perception may or may not be accurate are undertaken in chapter 10. Chapter 10 also investigates the extent to which immigrants receive Social Security income.

Discussion of findings, and conclusions are summarized in chapter 11. The chapter reviews results of the hypotheses tested, and discusses which theories are supported. Alternative explanations are given in the case of rejected theories. The final chapter (12) discusses implications and recommendations for U.S. immigration policy. These recommendations are provided in terms of feasibility and potential for success.

Chapter 2

Theoretical Perspectives on Immigration and the Labor Market

The most prominent explanations of the labor market effects of immigration stem from three general theories: human capital theory, dual labor market theory, and equilibrium theory. Each theory emphasizes some attribute or characteristic of the individual worker, for example, ability and skills, or labor market structure, for example discrimination, occupational hierarchy, or disparities in regional development. In this chapter, each of the three theories is reviewed. Their relevance to immigration and the labor market is also specified. Finally, appropriate hypotheses are derived.

The Human Capital Perspective

Human capital theory is essentially an explanation of earnings and other rewards that individuals receive from the labor market. The concept human capital refers to a collection of skills and abilities.

In its present form, the theory was proposed by Shultz (1961) and Becker (1975), and it views earnings as a monetary return on skills that an individual worker brings to the labor market. Jobs themselves do not play a significant role in the theory; they only provide a worker with the means by which his or her skills and abilities can be given their proper economic reward (Duncan, 1984:106).

The major assumptions of human capital theory are that the process of acquiring skills is costly, but at the same time, it is under the control of the individual worker. A second assumption is that although it takes time for workers to find jobs that best match their human capital, jobs are in abundance, and they are freely available to any person that has the right qualifications. The third and perhaps the most important assumption is that the major determinants of earnings are investments in schooling (education), or training and experience obtained while on the job (Lord and Falk, 1980). A further and related assumption is that education does not stop upon completion of formal schooling; instead, many necessary and important skills are learned on the job. Thus, individuals invest not only in classroom education, but in on-the-job training.

Proponents of human capital theory acknowledge that on-the-job training has its costs. Workers in training produce less than those that are not. As a consequence, labor market competition ensures that job trainees earn less than they would if they had jobs that did not demand additional training (Gerdes, 1977; Duncan, 1984). However, earning less is just temporary. The lower paying job is an investment in on-the-job training that eventually brings about higher earnings.

According to the human capital approach, it is up to the individual, as well as in his or her best interest to improve his or her competitive position in the labor market by increasing his or her productive capabilities. Investment in human capital is an investment that promises to bring about higher dividends. One way to maximize these labor market rewards is for the worker to invest early in life. Although initial rewards and earnings will be low, they will rise gradually.

Given the foregoing key assumptions and premises, the next issue to address is how the theory can be used to explain the performance of immigrants in the economy, and more importantly, their impact on the labor market.

One of the most important assumptions of human capital theory is that the primary determinants of a person's rate of pay are investments in schooling and on-the-job training. If the above assumption is correct, then it follows that whether or not an individual worker is an immigrant should not make a difference in earnings. Rather, investments in schooling and on-the-job training should make the most important differences in individual earnings. A hypothesis to derive from the foregoing reasoning is that immigrant status has no unique effects on earnings.

The main thrust of human capital theory is the rate of pay. However, earnings alone are not the only rewards derived by persons in the labor market. Although jobs may be in abundance, some have higher prestige than others, and persons occupying the higher prestigious jobs on average have higher earnings and higher socioeconomic attainment that others. Getting the higher prestigious jobs also entails some investment in human capital, and the higher one's investment, the higher one's occupational prestige and socioeconomic attainment. Accordingly, human capital interpretations would hypothesize that immigrant status has no unique effects on socioeconomic attainment and occupational prestige.

Human capital theory assumes that acquiring skills is under the individual worker's control. The question arises as to what happens in cases wherein the person concerned has failed to invest in his or her human capital. A number of things might happen. The individual may accept a job that pays very little, compared to what he or she would have earned had he or she invested. Another possibility is that he or she will become unemployed. It is thus, predicted that human capital variables will have significant negative effects on unemployment, and immigrant status will have no unique effects on unemployment.

Another possible consequence of failure to invest in human capital is that an individual may be forced to become economically dependent on others or on the public for sustenance. Accordingly, it is expected that human capital will have negative effects on public assistance use. Immigrant status will have no significant effects on the likelihood of public assistance use.

Implicit in the human capital approach is the view that employers hire workers solely on the basis of skills that they believe would maximize production and profits, regardless of race, sex, or national origin. To the extent that a significant number of immigrants posses skills deemed desirable by employers, and in places where immigrants have more of such skills than Americans, employers are more likely to favor hiring the former than the latter. If such a practice occurs on a large scale, competition between Americans (native born) and immigrants (foreign born) is likely to result. Employers might take advantage of such competition by reducing wages. The foregoing reasoning leads to the hypothesis that the higher the level of immigration, the lower the earnings of Americans. Relatedly, the higher the level of immigration, the lower the socioeconomic attainment and occupational prestige of Americans. The latter hypothesis is based on earlier arguments that workers derive other benefits from the labor market besides earnings.

Competition in the labor market leads not only to reduced earnings and lower socioeconomic attainment for Americans, but displacement. To the extent that competition is severe or immigrants posses higher human capital, some Americans are likely to lose jobs to immigrants. It is thus, predicted that the higher the level of immigration, the higher the American unemployment rate.

The Dual Labor Market Perspective

In contrast to human capital theory which focuses upon the skills of individual workers, dual labor market theory is concerned with the demand for workers, or the employer aspect of the labor market. It argues that there are institutional constraints that impede a freely competitive labor market (Duncan, 1984). Determinants of earnings and other labor market outcomes are sought in the characteristics of companies or firms that employ workers (Gordon, 1972; Edwards, 1975a; 1975b).

The key propositions of dual labor market theory are: (1) that economy is divided into two sectors: primary (or core/oligopoly) and secondary (or periphery), with little worker mobility between the two sectors (Doeringer and Piore, 1971). (2) Jobs in the primary sector are desirable because employees tend to receive higher wages, better promotional opportunities, and steady employment. (3) Earnings differences between the two sectors persist, regardless of education and other skills (Bonacich, 1972, 1976). These differences remain because employee payments reflect not only individual abilities, but the requirements of firms, as determined by specific production conditions. (4) Jobs in the primary sector have developed in stable and high wage industries in part through a process in which customary work rules and practices, formalized through collective bargaining, have established a separate market for persons already hired (Chang, 1989; Kerr, 1954; Duncan, 1984).

The secondary labor market has its own unique characteristics, among which is job instability. As Doeringer and Piore (1971:165-166) observed, jobs in the secondary sector "tend to have low wages and fringe benefits, poor working conditions, higher turnover, little chance of advancement, and often arbitrary and capricious supervision." Accordingly, there are no incentives for individual workers to remain with a particular employer; they respond to poor working conditions by frequently changing jobs. As Portes and Bach (1980:319) argue, "Segmentation of the economy along the competitive/oligopoly axis interacts with the pre-existing historical divisions by race, sex, and age in the labor market."

An outcome of the above division and accompanying labor market discrimination is that minorities, women, and new immigrants tend to be over represented in the secondary labor market, from which it is difficult to escape to the better paying jobs in the primary sector.
The collective vulnerability of these groups makes them a target used by firms to derive cheap labor and to keep wages down.

If the propositions of dual labor market theory are correct, then certain hypotheses can be inferred. First, presence of immigrants in the secondary labor market will generate competition between them and minorities. Competition will bring about earnings reduction or job loss for minorities. Employers will have a stronger bargaining power because supply of labor will exceed demand. This might force wages even lower. These observations lead to the hypothesis that the higher the level of immigration, the lower the earnings of minorities.

As already indicated, competition between immigrants and minorities in the secondary sector might also lead to job loss. If this is the case, it would be expected that the higher the level of immigration, the higher the minority unemployment rate.

Competition ensures that what is frequently a minority loss is a gain for the majority. Thus, even though minorities may lose jobs and obtain lower earnings on account of immigration, it is unlikely that the effects on the white majority will be identical. Higher immigration may, therefore, be positive for the majority. It is thus hypothesized that the higher the magnitude of immigration, the higher the industrial sector of Americans as a whole.

The Equilibrium Perspective

The third theoretical framework to examine is the equilibrium model of migration. Closely related to human capital theory, the equilibrium model explains migration as movement of workers responding to imbalances in the spatial distribution of land, labor, capital, and natural resources (Wood, 1982). Based on the classical labor mobility model, the equilibrium perspective holds that labor demand and supply are always in equilibrium, and labor adjusts according to the relative real wage rates and income between areas (Ritchey, 1976; Kposowa, 1986, 1987a). Migration of labor moves from areas where capital is scarce and labor in excess, to places where capital is abundant and labor is scarce. By redistributing workers from areas of low productivity to places of high productivity, migration becomes a process that corrects interregional or international imbalances in factor returns (Spengler and Myers, 1977). Migration of workers from less to more developed countries, especially evident in the last two decades, is a reflection of labor readjustment to market and production needs. Remittances sent by immigrants are seen as instrumental in restoring a balance of payments, and thereby stimulating savings and investment in the home (origin) country (Wood, 1982). Furthermore, should they return home, migrants promote change by applying ideas and skills acquired abroad to establish enterprises favorable to economic and societal development. From the perspective of the equilibrium model, international migration is positive because the movement of labor gradually brings about some sort of convergence in levels of economic growth and social well-being (Wood, 1982).

To maximize equilibrium, workers seek out those employment opportunities that offer them the greatest return. The equilibrium model assumes that migration is based on rational decisions by individuals who evaluate benefits to be gained as well as costs to be incurred in moving (Shaw, 1975; Sjaastad, 1962). In assessing the equilibrium model, analysts use variables such as information availability, costs of migration, distance between origin and potential destination, and the value of expected future income due to migration (Sjaastad, 1962; Rothenberg, 1977), and in developing countries, the probability of obtaining desirable employment in the modern sector (Harris and Todaro, 1970).

In examining the consequences of immigrants on American society, the equilibrium perspective might help explain why perhaps the effects of immigration are not uniform in the whole country. It may be that some states have better opportunities than others, and that it is the presence of such opportunities that draw immigrants to settle in them. Past suggestions in the literature that only a few states, (California, Florida, Illinois, New Jersey, New York, and Texas), have borne the full impact of immigration may very well be an affirmation of the equilibrium model. Recent research has also shown that the effect of immigration on receiving countries depend to a large extent on the opportunities available in sending countries. These opportunities determine type and quality of immigrant selection at origin (Borjas, 1994).

To avoid drawing spurious conclusions, it is important to ensure that any observed relationships between immigration and American earnings, socioeconomic attainment, or unemployment are not due to an uncontrolled third variable. A key assumption of equilibrium theory is that regional economic disparities account for higher levels of immigration into some regions than others. Implicit in this view is that there is a direct positive relationship between a region's level of economic development and its immigration level. A hypothesis to test based on equilibrium theory is that once regional economic development is controlled, immigration will have no effects on American earnings. A related hypothesis is that American earnings are determined exclusively by economic expansion.

Summary of Conceptual Hypotheses

1. Immigrant status has a significant effect on earnings.
2. Immigrant status has a significant effect on socio-economic attainment or occupational prestige.
3. Immigrant status has a significant negative effect on industrial sector.
4. Immigrant status has a significant positive effect on unemployment.
5. Immigrant status has a significant effect on public assistance.
6. The higher the level of immigration, the lower the earnings of Americans.
7. The higher the level of immigration, the lower the socioeconomic attainment and occupational prestige of Americans.

8. The larger the magnitude of immigration, the higher the American unemployment rate.

9. The higher the level of immigration, the higher the labor market sector of native born Americans.

10. Immigration has effects on native earnings even adjusting for economic expansion.

11. The greater the magnitude of immigration, the higher the native minority unemployment rate.

12. The higher the level of immigration, the lower the earnings of native minorities.

Chapter 3

Review of U.S. Immigration History and Previous Research

A Brief Survey of U.S. Immigration History

Immigration has played an important role in the population growth of the United States. Analysts say that even today, it accounts for over a quarter of the country's annual population growth rate (Carlson, 1985; Borjas, 1994). For over a century after the founding of the nation, there were no restrictions on immigration, except on persons classified as 'undesirables' with regard to their ethnic origins. The Alien and Sedition Act of 1798 set up the first federal statutory limits on immigration, but Congress failed to renew the act in 1800 (Bean, Vernez, and Keely, 1989).

In addition to the original settlers who landed in New England, millions of Africans migrated, albeit involuntarily between 1650 and 1800. Thus, African Americans rank among the earliest settlers of the United States. There is evidence that in fact Africans were in America at least one year before the Mayflower landed the Pilgrim Fathers at Plymouth Rock (Pinkney, 1993:2). Strangely and interestingly, however, Africans brought into slavery were not considered immigrants by the white population, a factor that latter had an important effect on future immigration of Africans to the United States after emancipation and well into the 1970s and 1980s. The involuntary nature of their entry (forced slavery) has been cited as the reason for the African exclusion. Subsequent U.S. immigration policies have demonstrated, however, that racial prejudice may have been a more accurate motive behind the classification of Americans of African descent as non-immigrants.

Since the founding of the United States, Western Europeans have dominated immigrant streams into the country. In fact, European immigrants and their descendants account for a substantial part of the U.S. population growth from the 4 million recorded in the 1790 census to its present levels (Bouvier, 1981, 1983). Prior to the Civil War, most immigrants came from Northern and Western Europe, notably Britain and Germany. The 1790 census reports that more than 75 percent of the population at that time had British ancestry.

Immigration increased markedly between 1800 and 1880, with over 80 percent of the newcomers coming from Northern and Western Europe (Carlson, 1985; Bouvier, 1983). Although England remained the dominant source of immigrants, by the 1870s, large numbers of immigrants were coming from other countries, including Germany, Ireland, France, Canada, Scotland and Sweden (Bean, Vernez, and Keely, 1989; Bouvier, 1983).

Federal involvement in, and control of immigration did not begin until the passage of the Immigration Act of 1875, which was notable for its exclusionary provisions. It barred the immigration of women for 'lewd or immoral' purposes, notably prostitution. It also proscribed immigration of persons undergoing a sentence for conviction in their own country of felonious crimes. Although the Immigration Act of 1875 did not preclude the entry of any persons on the basis of race or national origin it set the precedent for the infusion of national origin exclusions in subsequent legislation, beginning with the Chinese Exclusion Act of 1882. Passed following a series of debates and resolutions spanning the 40th Congress (1867-1869) to the 47th Congress (1881-1883), the Chinese Exclusion Act has been described by some observers as the first official policy to regulate immigration and restrict the entry of 'undesirable' ethnic groups (Li, 1976; 1981; Hutchinson, 1981). Among other things, the bill called for the deportation of any Chinese person found unlawfully in the United States, and barred state or other courts from admitting Chinese to citizenship.

The late 19th century saw dramatic changes in immigration with regard to ethnic origins. Southern and Eastern European countries replaced Northern and Western Europe as the new sources of most immigrants. In the 1890s, Italy was the leading source, and it was followed by Austria-Hungary, Russia, Poland, Turkey and Greece. From 1910 to 1919, Italy, Russia, Austria, and Hungary were the leading immigration sources, accounting for nearly two-thirds of immigrants (Carlson, 1985). Immigration from Southern and Eastern Europe became so massive (about 9 million entrants between 1900 and 1910 alone) that calls began to be heard from many Americans for restrictive congressional legislation (Abbott, 1926). It was believed by many Americans that earlier immigration policies had allowed too many immigrants from Southern and Eastern Europe. In addition, fears were expressed that should current trends continue, there could be serious political and social consequences for the United States. Earlier immigrants from Northern and Western Europe had been largely Protestant, but the new comers from Eastern and Southern Europe were predominantly Catholic.

Congress rose to the occasion with the passage of legislation in 1921 that limited immigration based upon nationality, and for the first time, numerical ceilings were imposed. Quotas of 3% per nationality groups were established, depending upon the number of foreign born residents in the 1910 census (Hutchinson, 1981). When quotas were combined, the total number of immigrants stood at no more than 350,000 per year from the eastern hemisphere. The western hemisphere was not subject to numerical ceilings and quotas (Briggs, 1984a; Carlson, 1985). Briggs (1984a:43) points out that the historical significance of the 1921 immigration act was that it represented the beginning of restrictions on immigration to the United States from Southern and Eastern Europe, Africa and Australia.

Congress passed a second immigration law in 1924, the Immigration and Naturalization Act or the National Origins Quota Act. It proved to be far more restrictive than the 1921 Immigration Act. The National Origins Act was in response to a widespread belief that in view of the already large size of foreign born populations from Southern and Eastern Europe, the 1921 legislation would have little or no effect. The 1924 Immigration and Naturalization Act set the quota for each country at 2% of its foreign born population in the United States, as reported in the 1890 census. A minimum quota of 100 immigrants was established for all qualifying countries (Hutchinson, 1981; Carlson, 1985; Briggs,

1984a). Since Northern and Western Europeans already had the largest number of foreign-born residents in 1890, the 1924 legislation appears to have been a deliberate attempt by Congress to favor Northern and Western Europe. The quota system excluded the descendants of African Americans, Native Americans, and of most Asians. In short, the beneficiaries of the 1924 National Origins Quota Act were whites of Northern and Western European descent. As Keely (1980) remarks, the basic assumptions of both the 1921 Immigration Act and the 1924 National Origins Act were clearly racist.

The 1924 Immigration and Naturalization Act made provision for the establishment of a system for determining national origin quotas for the future. That system allocated quotas to countries based upon one sixth of 1% of those white nationality (foreign-born and native-born) residents in the United States as recorded in the 1920 census (Carlson, 1985). Like before, countries in the Western hemisphere were exempt from quotas. By and large, the total number of immigrants entering under quotas was reduced to 160,000. Northern and Western European countries were allowed to have a larger share of quotas.

The 1924 Immigration act also established three categories of potential immigrants to the United States: quota immigrants, non-quota immigrants, and non-immigrants (Briggs, 1984a, 1984b). Quota immigrants are persons admitted for permanent residency. They can adjust their status and eventually become naturalized citizens. Non-quota immigrants are the spouses and unmarried children (under age 18) of those persons admitted as quota immigrants. Non-immigrants are those who enter on a temporary basis, for example, visitors, businessmen, crewmen, students, tourists, foreign government officials and representatives.

As a result of the Great Depression of the late 1920s and early 1930s, immigration to the United States declined to its lowest levels ever. It has been observed that between 1932 and 1935, more people emigrated from the U.S. than immigrated, and that five Mexicans left the country for every one that entered (Hoffman, 1978). It has been pointed out that in the twenty years following the introduction of the national origins system in 1929, only 27% of the existing quotas were used, and that immigration was only about 75% of the anticipated quota level (Briggs, 1984a:58).

The Second World War had several effects on U.S. immigration policy. The first had to do with labor. The U.S. was in need of farm laborers, and so in 1942, it initiated what became known as the Bracero Program. By its terms, under Public Law 45, and in agreement with the Mexican government, farm laborers from Mexico were permitted to enter and work in the U.S. on a temporary basis in agriculture. Contracts to individual immigrants ranged from forty-five days to six months. The entire program lasted from 1942 to 1964, and by the time it ended, more than four million Mexican workers had entered the United States (Cornelius, 1980). Bean, Vernez, and Keely (1989:7) comment that perhaps the most significant legacy of the Bracero Program for the United States was that what many Americans had assumed would be temporary migration frequently became permanent immigration.

The second effect of the war was that many U.S. military men had married to foreign women during the war. After the war, Congress passed the War Brides Act which made it possible for foreign spouses to join their husbands in the United States.

Finally, the Second World War created many humanitarian problems that had direct implications for U.S. immigration. Millions of people had been displaced as a result of the war, and they wanted to move to the United States. In response to this, Congress passed the Displaced Persons Act in 1948 (Keely, 1980). Both the War Brides Act and the Displaced Persons Act had provisions that lifted temporarily the restrictive quotas imposed by the National Origins Act (Keely, 1980; Briggs, 1984a). Consequently, immigration to the United States increased significantly after the Second World War. But like the National Origins Quota Act, both the Displaced Persons Act and the War Brides Act favored immigrants from Northern and Western Europe. The provisions of the new legislation called for 'mortgaging' the number of immigrants, up to 50 percent, against a country's future annual quotas (Carlson, 1985:311).

A persistent feature of the U.S. immigration system both prior to and after the Second World War was ethnic discrimination. While some countries in Western Europe, for example, had many unused quota slots each year, a backlog of potential immigrants waited to emigrate from other regions. As a result, calls began to be made for the conversion of the immigration system from one based on ethnic selectivity, to one that reflected the labor market needs of the country (Briggs, 1984b). There were also fears, following the Second World War that communists, fascists, and other 'subversive' elements were infiltrating the United States through the immigration system. In response to all the above, a U.S. Congress Senate Judiciary Committee conducted a review of the immigration process between 1947 and 1950 (U.S. Congress, Senate Committee on the Judiciary, 1950).

The Committee's recommendations led to passage of the Immigration and Nationality Act or the McCarran-Walter Act of 1952. Despite some minor modifications, the McCarran-Walter Act retained the basic principles of existing immigration laws. The national origins system favoring Europe was maintained, as well as the total ceiling for the Eastern Hemisphere set at 154,277 immigrants. Although the Act removed exclusions of Asians, provisions for administering quotas for them were more restrictive than those applied to Europeans. As Briggs (1984a:58) points out, the act was essentially a reaffirmation of the main principles that had prevailed since the 1920s.

A new and important feature of the McCarran-Walter Act was that it created a preference system by which to distribute visas within the quota allotments assigned to each country. Four categories of preference were established. In the first, half of the visas issued under each quota allotment were to be given to workers with a level of education, technical training, special experiences, or exceptional abilities that were judged by the attorney-general to be of benefit to the United States (Briggs, 1984a:58). Other levels of preference gave priority to various categories of relatives of citizens or permanent-resident aliens.

Another significant feature of the McCarran-Walter Immigration Act was that it initiated labor certification as a requirement for the admission of immigrants. It was left to the labor secretary to certify that the admission of non-relative immigrants would not have an adverse effect on wages and working conditions of native workers employed in similar occupations. The Department of Labor could refuse certification if in its judgement an adverse effect would occur.

As the 1950s drew to a close, U.S. immigration laws were still racially and ethnically discriminatory. Furthermore, as the President's Commission on Immigration and Naturalization (1953:263) had indicated, the laws were based upon an attitude of hostility and distrust of foreigners, and they were difficult to administer. In the early 1960's various amendments were made to the McCarran-Walter Immigration

Act of 1952. These amendments were passed as the 1965 Amendments to the Immigration and Nationality Act, or the Hart-Celler Immigration Act (U.S. Bureau of the Census, 1990:B-3; Harper, 1975). This Act has been described as the most comprehensive revision of U.S. immigration policy since the imposition of the first numerical quotas in 1921. Briggs (1984a:61) argues that:

> Since its passage, immigration to the United States has changed dramatically both quantitatively and qualitatively. The re-emergence of immigration as a significant labor market influence virtually dates from the implementation of this legislation.

The Immigration and Nationality Act of 1965 amended the U.S. immigration system in several important ways. For the first time, a ceiling was imposed on the number of entrants from the Western Hemisphere. This was done out of congressional fears that the absence of a limit in the face of high population growth rates in Latin America, would lead to a huge influx of immigrants in the future (Harper, 1975). A ceiling of 120,000 was set.

Perhaps the most important aspect of the 1965 Amendments to the Immigration and Nationality Act was the abolishment of the discriminatory national origins system. Under the new legislation, although country of origin remained a basic policy component, preference could not be given on the basis of race, sex, place of birth, or place of origin (Briggs, 1984a:63). Kinship ties with U.S. citizens or permanent resident aliens (instead of labor market considerations) was established as the new criteria for issuing visas.

The Immigration and Nationality Act of 1965 placed an annual ceiling of 170,000 visas on all the countries of the Eastern Hemisphere combined. This figure, when combined with the Western Hemisphere ceiling of 120,000 ensured that the total number of visas to be issued each year was up to 290,000. A ceiling of 20,000 visas per any one country was also established (U.S. Bureau of the Census, 1990:B-3).

The 1965 Immigration and Nationality Act remained the basis of the U.S. immigration system from 1965 to the 1980s, although some amendments and modifications were made in the 1970s. In the 1980s,

Chapter Three

however, the perception grew that illegal immigration was becoming a serious national problem. As a result, pressures mounted for legislation to stop illegal flows. One of the most tangible results of these pressures was the Immigration Reform and Control Act (IRCA) of 1986.

The Immigration Reform and Control Act was aimed at achieving several things. Among these were to: 1) Curtail illegal immigration; 2) Adjust or legalize the status of 'qualified' illegal aliens already in the United States; 3) Ensure that labor demands in agriculture were met, and 4) protect citizens and legal immigrants against employment discrimination (U. S. Congress, 1986). As passed by the Congress (U.S. Congress, 1986) IRCA has eight major provisions:

1.   Employer Requirements and Sanctions.
      The Act made it a crime to hire undocumented workers.
2.   Anti-discrimination Safeguards.
      Under this provision, it became illegal for employers to discriminate against foreign-looking or foreign sounding citizens and legal aliens.
3.   A Legalized Authorized Workers Program (laws).
      This program adjusted or legalized the status of aliens that had been in continuous residence in the United States since 1982.
4.   A Special Agricultural Workers Legalization Program (saws).
      Under its provisions, the status of aliens who had worked in agriculture up through 1986 was adjusted.
5.   A Replenishment Program.
      This sought to grant further entry to additional immigrants for work in agriculture after 1990, if newly legalized immigrants under the previous provision moved out of the agricultural sector.
6.   A State Legalization Impact Assistance Grants Program (SLAG).
      By the terms of this provision, the federal government agreed to pay states for additional costs associated with legalization over a period of four years.
7.   A Systematic Alien Verification for Entitlements Program (SAVE).The above determines the eligibility of non-citizens for public assistance programs that are financed by the federal government.
8.   Increased Enforcement.
      The Act provided more funds for the U. S. Immigration and Naturalization Service (INS), and the U.S. Department of Labor.

Since the passage of the Immigration Reform and Control Act of 1986, there have been calls for reforms of policies on legal immigration as well (Bean, Vernez, and Keely, 1989:25-26). It is yet unknown how those reforms will affect the U.S. immigration system.
Early Indications in the late 1980s and early 1990s suggest that it has not had any significant impact.

Geographic Distribution of Immigrants

With regard to labor market effects of immigration, an issue frequently raised is that the geographic distribution of immigrants, especially post 1965 is regionally unbalanced. Five states seem to account for nearly two thirds of the country's immigrants (Bouvier, 1983; Bach and Tienda 1984). Since the 1970s, California has emerged as the largest receiver of legal immigrants, followed by New York, which was once the largest receiver. California and New York combined receive between 40 and 45 percent of all legal immigrants (Greenwood, 1983; Bach and Tienda, 1984). Other high immigrant destinations are Texas, Florida, Illinois and New Jersey.

North and Weisberg (1974:67) have shown that in the states they settle, immigrants tend to be drawn to large urban areas. It is estimated that a central city was the destination of about 55% of the immigrants admitted between 1960 and 1979. Next in preference for immigrants were suburban areas with a population between 2,500 and 99,000. Rural areas have generally lagged behind urban areas in destination preferences for immigrants (U.S. Department of Justice, Immigration and Naturalization Service, 1982:31).

Possible consequences of the geographic concentration of immigrants in urban centers of a few states have been investigated by analysts. Defrauds and Marshall (1984), in an analysis of 1980 U.S. census data observed that one-third of all foreign-born workers were employed in manufacturing, compared to 23% of native-born workers. They also found that 75% of all workers employed in manufacturing in Miami were immigrants, and so were 40% of those in Los Angeles and New York City, 25% in San Francisco, and 20% in Chicago and Boston. Defrauds and Marshall looked at thirty-five metropolitan areas of the nation with populations of one million or more and found that the rate of wage growth in manufacturing was negatively related to the size of the immigrant population of those areas. Thus, as Briggs (1984a:58) comments, "Only a few states and a handful of cities have borne the brunt of the revival of immigration that has occurred since 1965."

Change in Countries of Origin (The 'New Immigration')

One of the most dramatic results of the 1965 Immigration and Nationality Act was that its abolishment of the national-origins system led to a complete shift in the major regions of origin of immigrants. Bouvier (1981) shows that since the 1970s, countries in Latin America and Asia have become the primary sources of U.S. immigrants. He further indicates that since the decade of the 1960s, Latin America has replaced Europe as the leading source of immigrants to the United States. Data from the U.S. Immigration and Naturalization Service (U.S. Department of Justice, 1993) support the above observation. They further show that the pattern has continued into the 1980s and 1990s.

Reasons for this regional shift are obvious. Until passage of the Immigration and Nationality Act of 1965, immigration from Latin America was not subject to quotas. Hence there was opportunity for individuals from there to move to the United States and later use their presence to reunify their families through the admission of relatives (Bean, Telles and Lowell, 1987). The case for Asians is less clear, especially in view of past policies specifically designed to discourage their immigration. It is probable, however, that the refugee provisions of the immigration system has benefitted Asians. Briggs (1984a:79) says that as a consequence of the Vietnam war, over half a million refugees were admitted from Southeast Asia between 1975 and 1981. The refugees came from Vietnam, Kampuchea, and Laos. In addition, legal immigration also brought people from the Philippines, Taiwan, Korea, India and Hong Kong.

Effects of Immigration on the United States Labor Market

Competition and Displacement

As early as 1953, Bernard (1953:57) challenged the notion that immigrant workers displace native workers in the labor market. He wrote:

> One of the most persistent and recurrent fallacies in popular thought is the notion that immigrants take away the jobs of native

> Americans. This rests on the misconception
> that only a fixed number of jobs exist in any
> economy and that any newcomer threatens the
> job of any old resident.

Bernard added that job opportunities in any country are not fixed at a particular level. Rather such opportunities expand as the population increases. A number of factors account for the expansion in opportunities. According to Bernard, since immigrants are consumers, they bring about an expansion in the labor market. They also encourage increased investment expenditures, and in so doing, they contribute to increased total demand for goods and services. Bernard argued that immigrants make important contributions to technological progress and entrepreneurial activity.

Despite Bernard's persuasive arguments, there is still persistent belief in the United States that immigration has detrimental effects on the U.S. labor market. One basic argument is that immigrants, especially illegals, enter the United States mainly for economic reasons, and that better job opportunities are available to them at their destination, compared to opportunities in their own country (Greenwood, 1983). Consequently, the argument goes on, they compete with, and displace native workers. However, as Greenwood (1983:239) indicates, even among analysts studying the problem of illegal immigration, there is widespread disagreement concerning the effects of immigration on domestic workers.

Reder (1963:227) argued that immigration had had serious consequences on the U.S. labor market. He wrote:

> A greater flow of immigration will injure labor
> market competitors with immigrants; these are,
> predominantly Negroes, Puerto Ricans,
> unskilled immigrants able to enter the country,
> and native rural-urban migrants.

Reder further claimed that increased immigration caused labor market substitution for secondary earners, such as married women, youths and the elderly. According to him, in addition to affecting employment opportunities of domestic workers, immigrants depress the annual earnings of those native workers with whom they are in competition. On the other hand, native workers, such as supervisors, who are complementary to the immigrant workers benefit in terms of higher earnings. Reder suggests that since immigration retards rural to urban migration, rural residents with already low incomes are worst affected. He reasons that farm labor supply will be larger than it otherwise would be, which puts a downward pressure on farm wages.

Muth (1971:295) found that the effect on employment of an additional worker is about equal to 1.0. He concluded that immigration seems to induce an increase in employment almost proportionate to its expected increase in a city's labor force. Briggs (1975a, 1975b) put forward a 'replacement hypothesis' in which he claimed that aliens depress local wage levels and take jobs that would otherwise be held by domestic workers. As evidence, he argued that:

> The bracero program depressed domestic wage rates and retarded the normal market pressures that would have led to rising agricultural wages in the Southwest...Their level, relative to wages in the non-agricultural sectors, declined sharply. Since the end of the bracero program, the illegal immigrants have had the same effect (Briggs, 1975a:358).

Other researchers have adopted a position that seems to contradict that of Briggs, and have proposed what may be described as a 'segmentation hypothesis'. Abrams and Abrams (1975:25) argued that the jobs filled by illegal aliens are not at the expense of native workers. They pointed out:

> As to the assertion that illegal aliens take jobs away from Americans, there is a ... lack of evidence. Certainly, it is not logical to conclude that if they are actually employed they are taking a job away from one of our American citizens (Abrams and Abrams, 1975:25).

Abrams and Abrams seem to suggest that the labor market is segmented such that native workers are insulated from the direct employment effects of immigrants. A further argument against the replacement hypothesis of Briggs, and in favor of the segmentation hypothesis of Abrams and Abrams was offered by Piore (1979). He said that in advanced industrial societies, some jobs are undesirable to the native work force. He adds that:

> The jobs tend to be unskilled, generally but not always low paying, and to carry or connote inferior social status; they often involve hard or unpleasant working conditions and considerable insecurity; they seldom offer chances of advancement toward better-paying, more attractive opportunities (Piore, 1979:17).

As a result of the existing demand for the types of employment Piore concluded that an immigrant work force develops and thrives.

Johnson (1980:331) affirmed that immigrants compete directly with the domestic population in the labor market, and that the latter would in the short run be worse off due to additional immigration. In an analysis of 'hypothetical' data, he concluded that a high rate of immigration of low-skilled labor into the United States has a rather large effect on the distribution of income. He added that low-skilled workers would lose as a result of immigration, largely through lower wages rather than increased unemployment. Johnson further pointed out that the additional low-skilled labor that results from immigration raises the earnings of high-skilled workers and owners of capital.

Wachter (1980:343) suggested that in the 1980s, as the native labor force declined, an increased immigrant flow would benefit skilled older workers and owners of capital. He argued that whereas skilled workers would benefit from increased immigration, unskilled workers would suffer from it. Their relative income would be lowered, and their unemployment rates would rise.

Li (1981) challenged the notion that immigrants displace native workers. Using regression analysis on data from the 1976 Survey of Income and Education, he contradicted the assumption that immigrants and minority workers are engaged in direct economic competition. Li affirmed that immigrants are more likely to take jobs that fall between the disparate occupational distributions of minority and white workers. He concluded that:

> Immigrants seem to play a role that is complementary to either side of the social spectrum in a host society. Therefore, to assume that immigrants directly compete with a particular social group will be an overstatement (Li, 1981:166).

He admitted, however, that immigrants and minority workers may be in competitive positions in certain sectors of the economy, but such jobs represent only a small portion of the total occupational spectrum. Li concluded that the "frequent allegation that immigrants take jobs away from natives appears to be a simplistic exaggeration, meaningful only at a one-to-one level" (Li, 1981:167).

Grossman (1982) used a translog production function to determine substitution effects between capital, the stock of immigrants in the United States, and the native labor force in 1970. He divided the native work force into second generation (or sons of immigrants) and third generation (all other immigrants). Grossman found that immigrants and both second- and third- generation workers are only slight substitutes in production. Even after including capital in the model, it did not have any effects on the results. He found that all labor groups are substitutes for one another, but that immigrant inflows affect established natives's wages only slightly. He added that second generation immigrants and established natives are much closer substitutes. Grossman's results showed that moderately large inflows of immigrants did not pose serious economic threats to natives, although their effects were not negligible. He wrote that "the fear of economic displacement that is observed in some parts of the country may come from the uneven distribution of immigrants" (p. 602). Grossman thus recommended that immigration policy should aim at encouraging the dispersion of new immigrants around the country so as to minimize the detrimental economic effects on the native population.

Bean, Telles and Lowell (1987:683) cautioned, however, that results from Grossman's study may not apply to Mexican or illegal immigrants because the stock of all immigrants in the study is primarily legal, better educated, comprises many nationalities, has lived in the United States for more years, and is dispersed into more labor markets. Bean and his companions further advise that the Grossman study failed to control for differences in skill levels, and thus his results compare quite different groups that might rarely, if ever, compete in the labor market.

Briggs (1984b) argued that illegal immigrant workers are concentrated in the secondary labor market of the U.S. economy. He went on to say that within this labor market, they often compete with the millions of citizen workers who also work or seek work in this sector. Briggs said that the occupational impact of legal immigrants is at the upper end of the nation's occupation structure while that of illegal aliens is at the lower end. He cautioned that studies which combine the two groups to obtain an average measure of the experience of immigrants on the labor force underestimate the significance of the true impact. Briggs concludes that in the short run, immigrants probably contribute to higher unemployment rates.

Simon and Moore (1984) examined the effects of immigration on unemployment. In particular, they were interested in how differences in immigration patterns into cities is related to changes in unemployment across various cities. Using regression techniques, the researchers built a three-year lag between immigration and unemployment into their model, arguing that it provided the most critical test of the labor market's ability to adjust. They concluded that immigration produces little or no displacement. However, the General Accounting Office (1986), using a different lag suggested that aliens displace native workers.

Marshall (1984:602) proposed that the economic effects of immigration depends on labor market conditions in the United States and the characteristics of immigrants. He pointed out that if immigrant workers lack skills that are in short supply, and if unemployment is high in areas where immigrants concentrate, then immigration is more likely to have adverse effects on the labor market.

Bach and Tienda (1984) found in their analysis of 1980 census data a process of immigrant succession. Their findings, based on 'shift share analysis' showed that immigrants fill jobs being vacated by domestic workers. They commented on a pattern of bifurcation in the occupational structure of immigrants. Hispanic immigrants tended to concentrate in low status occupations, while Asian immigrants were in higher status ones. Using a generalized Leontief production function, Borjas (1984:85) broke down the labor force into various groups in order to assess the issue of substitutability among them. He found that male immigrants, as a single group did not generally have a negative impact on the earnings of any male-born group in the United States, whether black or white. His results suggested that in fact, male immigrants may have had a small positive effect on the earnings of native-born men in the labor market. Results for women were, however, different. Borjas noted that female immigrants and native-born men seem to be substitutes in production, such that an increase in the number of female immigrants in the labor market is detrimental to earnings of male native workers. He cautioned, however, that this finding is not unique since women and men seem to be strong substitutes in production, regardless of immigration status. Borjas further found that different types of male immigrants appear to have a differential impact on the earnings of the native-born. Non-Hispanic immigrants had a strong positive effect on the earnings of natives, but Hispanic immigrants had neither a positive nor a negative effect. Borjas concluded that "...the labor market benefits accruing to the male native-born population from immigration are due mostly to the immigration of non-Hispanics into the United States" (p. 116).

Borjas (1987:382) re-examined the issue of labor market competition between immigrants and minority workers. He criticized previous research for concluding that immigrants have a very small numerical impact on the earnings of the native population. Borjas charged that past studies had failed to disaggregate rather different immigrant groups. He said that:

> Since it is well known that the national origin
> of the immigrant population ... is an important
> characteristic in the determination of earnings,
> the conclusion that immigrants have had little
> impact on native earnings may well be masking
> important country- or race-specific distinctions
> in the extent of substitutability (Borjas,
> 1987:383).

He went on to estimate the extent of labor market competition between immigrants and natives in which both groups are disaggregated by race and ethnic origins. Using data from the 1980 census, Borjas (1987) obtained results similar to Grossman's 1982 study, but contrary to Li's 1981 study. Borjas found that in general, immigrants tend to be substitutes for some labor market groups and complements for others. He observed that white native-born men are adversely affected by increases in immigration. Borjas concluded that immigrants have not played a major role in the determination of wage levels for native-born men in recent years. Thus, while in his 1984 study Borjas reported that immigrants did not have negative effects on the labor market, in his 1987 research, they now seemed to have detrimental impacts.

Borjas and Tienda (1987:645-650) assessed the economic consequences of immigrants and concluded that the negative effects of immigrants on the earnings of native workers are quite small. The authors added that despite increases in the volume of immigration in recent decades, it has not exceeded the growth rate or absorptive capacity of the U.S. labor force. Borjas and Tienda also argued against the assumption that immigrants compete with and displace native workers. With some qualifications, they indicated that available evidence is inconsistent with charges that immigrants impose major cost on the U.S. because they reduce the earnings of native workers.

Matta and Popp (1988:105-116) examined the effects of immigrants on the earnings of youth in the United States. Using data from the 1976 Survey of Income and Education (SIE), they found that immigration does affect the earnings of youth, but the effect is very small. They reported that for the whole sample, a one percentage point increase in immigration proportion reduces earnings by .723 percent. Matta and Popp also found that negative and larger impacts of immigration are due to the presence of more recently arrived immigrants. They reported that the higher the percentage of recently arrived immigrants in a give labor market, the lower the earnings of youth. They concluded that post 1968 immigrants and native-born youth labor are gross substitutes in the labor market.

Immigrant Concentration

Although the impact of immigration may be hard to see at the national level, its effects may be more dramatic at local levels. North and LeBel (1978) identified ten cities which they alleged were seriously affected by immigration. The cities included New York, Los Angeles,

Chicago, Miami, San Francisco, Honolulu, Houston, Newark, El Paso, and Philadelphia. These cities were ranked with reference to the number of arriving immigrants who chose them as their initial destination.

Smith and Newman (1977) examined the possibility that detrimental effects of immigration may be best studied by focusing on regions having large concentrations of immigrants. To do this, they looked at income differentials along the U.S. Mexican border. After controlling for various socioeconomic and demographic factors, they reported that the nominal income differential between border and non border regions was $1,680 (or 20 percent). The real differential in favor of non border areas was $684, (or 8 percent). They found that border areas with heavier concentrations of Mexican-Americans are more adversely affected than those with lighter concentrations. In giving specific examples, Smith and Newman reported that Laredo, a border region with about 85 percent Mexican-American population, suffers a real income loss of $1,272, compared to Houston, a non border area with a population that was approximately 9% Mexican-American. Greenwood (1983:243) reported that:

> For New York, Los Angeles, Chicago, Miami, and San Francisco, one more employed migrant results in one more job ... For Houston, El Paso, Philadelphia, and San Diego, one additional employed migrant resulted in more than one additional job.

Todaro concluded that in addition to affecting local employment levels, the typical employed migrant affected local wage or earnings levels. He added that in each city, except El Paso and Philadelphia, immigration has a statistically significant effect on local earnings levels. This effect was positive in all cities, except in Chicago where it was negative.

Immigrants, Wages, and Wage Depression

A common perception in regard to immigration is that illegal immigrants cause competition in the labor market which in turn leads to reduced wages and earnings for natives. Representing this view are Briggs (1984a, 1984b) and Marshall (1987). Both see immigrants as competing with natives for jobs and also of being a source of labor supply that deprives natives of employment and earnings. Implicit in the argument of both men is that immigrants and native workers compete in a similar or unified labor market for employment and wages. Domestic youth, women and minorities are often depicted as being most severely hurt (Bean et al., 1987). Briggs and Marshall basically see immigrants as a source of competition that jeopardizes the jobs and earnings of domestic workers.

Another view portrays immigrants as a low-skilled labor pool that fills jobs that native workers will not accept. It is argued that in the absence of immigrants, such jobs might disappear, either due to capital substitution or their exportation to more labor intensive nations (Piore, 1979). Implied in this argument is that the wages of natives are little influenced by the presence of immigrant workers. Bean, Telles, and Lowell (1987:677) comment that:

> It may be hypothesized that the real wages of natives are increased by the presence of low-skilled and undocumented immigrants who provide goods and services to the native community at lower prices than would otherwise prevail, and who save (and perhaps create) the jobs of supervisory and complementary workers (who are likely to be natives) in industries requiring cheap labor for their survival.

Van Arsdol, Moore, Heer, and Haynie (1979) concluded from a study of the Hispanic population that illegal male immigrants do not compete with other labor force groups. This was in contradiction to a study by North and Houston (1976) which suggested that illegal immigrants tend to cluster in specific geographic areas in which they compete with and displace native workers. As a result, they concluded that native workers with low skills in these same areas experience lower wages and poorer working conditions.

Maram (1980), in a survey of owners and managers found that regardless of legal status, immigrants had negative effects, but only on the wages of other immigrants in the restaurant industry. However, illegal immigrants in the restaurant industry depressed the wages of most other workers.

Vasquez (1981) reported wage depression in the Los Angeles cloth industry. However, other research of the garment, restaurant and construction industries in the New York metropolitan area failed to find evidence in support of significant depression of domestic worker wages (Waldinger, 1983; Bailey, 1987). Waldinger (1983) and Bailey (1987) reported that immigrants tend to be concentrated in menial and physically difficult jobs that are clearly distinct from jobs held by domestic workers. However, in a study of Brownsville, Texas, Miller (1981) found a sharp rise in unemployment and a drop in the real wages of low-skilled native workers as a result of immigration from Mexico.

Wise (1974) found that the ending of the bracero program in 1964, which meant a halt to cheap labor from Mexico, markedly increased domestic employment and wages, while reducing production in the California strawberry and winter melon industries. However, a more recent study by Mines and Anzaldua (1982) of the California citrus industry, found little evidence of job displacement by temporary workers, mostly illegal immigrants.

McCarthy and Valdez (1986) using data from the 1970 and 1980 censuses of population observed little negative effects of immigration on the wages of domestic workers, but they found that the wages of Hispanic workers grew at less than the national average rate between 1970 and 1980. They argued that immigration from Mexico served to improve working conditions and employment opportunities of native workers by providing a boost to otherwise failing, low-wage industries. The authors, however, failed to take into account other factors that might affect earnings of native workers.

Muller and Espenshade (1985) used regression analysis on 1970 and 1980 U.S. census data to examine differences in black family income due to immigration across labor markets. Differences were explained by using such variables as percentage Hispanic in 51 Southwest Standard Metropolitan Sampling Areas (SMSAs), population growth from 1970 to 1980, percentage income in construction and durable goods manufacturing, percentage black completing 12 years of schooling, and white income. The latter was used as a control variable to index local economic factors affecting all workers. Percentage Hispanic was used as an indicator of Mexican immigration. The researchers found that for the country as a whole, the Hispanic population has a small negative effect on income, while in the Southwest, a positive relation was found for percentage Mexican born. They concluded that the effect on black family income is small.

Cornelius (1978) argued that illegal immigrants experience little wage discrimination as such, but they receive lower wages because they are younger, and have lower educational levels, compared to legal immigrants and natives. Illegal immigrants also have less work experience and lower competence in English than legal immigrants. Cornelius's work thus suggests that low human capital, and not immigrant status as such, may explain lower wages among immigrants.

Briggs (1975a, 1984a, 1984b) on the other hand argued that immigrants are a 'shadow labor force' that is easily exploited and receives lower wages as a result. Commenting on the views of Cornelius and Briggs, Massey (1987) affirms that which ever one is correct has important implications for the effects of immigration on wage rates. If Cornelius' view is accurate, then increases in illegal immigrants should not affect wage rates, but may increase the supply of foreign labor. On the other hand, if Briggs is correct, then an increase in illegal aliens should bring down wages (Bean, Telles and Lowell, 1987).

Borjas (1986) investigated whether estimates of cross-sectional labor demand functions are sensitive to the method of estimation that accounts for change. He sought to determine whether an analysis of cross-sections at two points in time would better explain demographic change within labor markets than a simple comparison between labor markets in which an event occurred and those in which it did not. Among other things, he concluded that immigrant males have negative effects on domestic workers, but such effects are minimal.

Borjas (1987) divided the labor market by race and nationality and found immigrants having relatively small negative effects on domestic workers. He observed that white native men were the most adversely affected by increases in immigrant workers. On the other hand, native black males experienced a slight gain. Borjas also reported that an increase in the supply of each of the various groups of Hispanics had small effects on the earnings of non-Hispanics, but considerable effects on the earnings of the Hispanic groups themselves.

King, Lowell and Bean (1986) used both a Leontief production function and a human capital model to specify equations on earnings.

They used 1970 data to examine the impact of immigrant Hispanic workers on the earnings of second and third generation Hispanics. They found that native Hispanic workers employed in labor markets that have higher concentrations of Hispanic workers did not fare significantly worse than natives in labor markets less populated by immigrants. In the case of unskilled laborers, however, a slight negative effect was observed.

Bean, Lowell and Taylor (1988) examined the effects of undocumented Mexican immigrants on the earnings of other workers in geographic labor markets in the southwestern United States. They estimated the parameters of three specifications of a generalized Leontief production function with various demographic groups as substitutable factors. Bean, Lowell, and Taylor (1988) found that illegal immigrants had little effect on the earnings of individuals in each of five other labor force groups. They also found that legal immigrants' effects on native white earnings are small and negative. They concluded that their results are consistent with the possibility that illegal Mexican immigrants' jobs complement those of other workers. The authors reported that the supply of legal Mexican workers exhibits a negative effect on female earnings. They pointed out that the earnings of black as well as native Mexican workers were not significantly affected by the number of illegal immigrant workers in local labor markets. They commented that the latter finding was especially interesting, since black and native Hispanic minorities are believed to work in industries most affected by illegal alien workers. Bean and his companions argued that their findings suggest that illegal immigrants hold jobs that others despise. They added that their findings are less consistent with the view that illegal immigrants compete with natives especially minorities for jobs and wages.

Immigration and Economic Dependence

A final, but crucial issue relating to the impact of immigration on the labor market and the general economic health of the United States is the relationship between immigration and public assistance utilization. Do immigrants receive welfare income financed by federal and state taxes, or do they contribute to the U.S. economy more my working and paying taxes than what they take away from it.

Despite the significance of the above issue and the ongoing national controversy surrounding it, very little research has been done to address it. Simon (1984) studied what he described as the balance of transfers between immigrant groups and natives based on data from the 1976 Survey of Income and Education. He found that in every year following entry, "immigrants benefit native workers through the public coffers, and that the average immigrant is an excellent investment for U.S. tax payers" (p. 66). Simon observed that the net balance of taxes paid and services received by immigrants has a positive impact on natives. He concluded that immigrants contribute more to the public coffers than they take from it.

Blau (1984) examined the effects of immigration on the use of transfer payments. In addition, she was interested in the relevance of transfer payment utilization of two immigrant characteristics: duration of residence in the United States, and proficiency in the English language. Blau's results revealed that total transfer payments to an immigrant family were higher on average than to a native family. In addition, they showed that immigrant families were considerably less likely to rely on welfare than native families with similar characteristics. Blau affirmed that the total expected transfer payments to male-headed immigrant families were the same as payments to comparable native families. She added that observed differences between immigrant and native families with regard to use of transfer payments are due to group differences in characteristics, or ways in which immigrant and native families differ from each other. Her findings also indicated that immigrant-native differences in age-related variables are enough to account for all of the higher use of transfer by immigrant families. Unlike natives, the age distribution of immigrants tend to be a function of historical trends in immigration, rather than fertility or mortality. Immigrants are, therefore, older than natives, and their age increases their use of transfer payments. Blau concluded than since the majority of older immigrants have spent most of their lives in the United States, and have working age children contributing taxes to finance social programs, their higher dependence on transfers for age-related reasons does not constitute an undue burden on the transfer payment program.

Weintraub (1984) used data from a survey of 253 illegal immigrants in an investigation of the effects of illegal immigration on social and related services in Texas. He found that illegal immigrants use public services, mainly education and health, but they rarely receive welfare services such as AFDC and food stamps. Weintraub's findings further showed that the state of Texas receives more from taxes paid by illegal immigrants than the cost incurred by the state to provide them with public services, such as education, health care, corrections, and welfare. However, he found that six cities in Texas, Austin, Dallas, El Paso, Houston, McAllen, and San Antonio spent more to provide services to undocumented aliens than they received in taxes.

Tienda and Jensen (1986) used 1980 census data to examine the problem of immigrants and transfer income utilization. Their results showed that despite marginally higher than average participation of immigrants in public assistance income, immigrants were much less likely than native whites to become welfare recipients. Their findings seemed to dispel allegations that new immigrants participate in welfare programs. Tienda and Jensen found, however, that Asian immigrants who arrived after 1974 were significantly likely to receive public assistance.

Similar findings were reported by Borjas and Trejo (1991) who found that immigrants arriving after the 1970s were significantly more likely to receive public assistance. They further indicated that immigrants from developing countries were also more likely to be on public assistance, compared to immigrants from more developed countries. Their findings seem to link the likelihood of public assistance to 'immigrant quality', and its presumed decline following 1965.

The foregoing review illustrates that the literature on the effects of immigration on the U.S. labor market is quite inconsistent and contradictory. Some studies have found that immigrants compete with, and displace native workers. Others have provided evidence against displacement and competition. Research which appeared to establish immigration as a depressing factor of wages has in turn been challenged. Furthermore, the nature of the impact of immigrants on public assistance use is still unclear.

The present research in part begins to explore explanations for discrepancies observed in the past literature. It suggests that some of the inconsistent findings and contradictions are due to the reliance on examining immigration's effects at only specific points of time, and on relying on earnings as the sole indicator of labor market outcomes. Analysis of trend data in the present research should enable us to determine whether some of the contradictions present in past research are results of studying immigration using only cross-sectional designs.

Chapter 4

Materials and Methods

Nature and Source of Data

The data utilized in this research were derived from two sources. The first set of data was the *United States Microdata Samples Extract File, 1940-1980: The Demographics of Aging* (henceforth referred to as the *Demographics of Aging File*). It was made available in part by the Inter-University Consortium for Political and Social Research (ICPSR). The data were collected by the United States Bureau of the Census (ICPSR, 1987). The special subset of the data employed was prepared by the National Archive Computerized Data on Aging (NACDA) under support from the National Institute on Aging.

The data set comprises five files from the Public Use Microdata samples (PUMS) for 1940, 1950, 1960, 1970, and 1980. The original sampling was accomplished by selecting households from internal census basic record tapes (ICPSR, 1987). *The Demographics of Aging File* is especially useful for cohort or trend analysis. The 1970 is helpful in understanding the impact of immigration following the 1965 Amendments to the Immigration and Nationality Act, while the 1980 sample reveals the nature of immigration following the collapse of U.S. sponsored regimes in Indo-China.

The second source of data is the 1 percent Public Use Microdata (B) Sample of the 1980 Census of Population and Housing (U.S. Bureau of the Census, 1983a). The Sample selected include one percent of all persons aged 16 to 64, occupied in civilian jobs at the time of the census.

To summarize, the data for this research were drawn from the individual records in both the *Demographics of Aging File*, and the 1 in 100 Public Use Sample of the 1980 Census. Records with allocated nationality were deleted. Allocation is an editing process devised by the U.S. Census Bureau to assign information that was originally absent on a census questionnaire. Cases in the analysis from the Demographics of Aging File consist of persons aged 18 to 64 the in census year. In the 1980 Public Use Sample, cases analyzed are those age 16 to 64.

The analysis covers the period from 1940 to 1980. Such a time span has advantages as well as disadvantages. The major advantage is that it allows us to investigate dynamic aspects and trends of the immigration issue. In other words, focusing on a long time span will show whether the effects of immigration observed during a particular decade are invariant with those noted in other periods. Second, a longitudinal design as opposed to a cross-sectional (one-shot) design may reveal what factors were especially at work within a specific period, and how political, social, historical, economic, and legal factors operating at various points in time influenced immigration. The design adopted here may enlighten us as to whether immigrants arriving within a given decade affect the labor market negatively, and if such effects hold true for all immigrants regardless of their time of entry. Put differently, the analysis attempts to show whether the alleged negative effects of immigration (if they exist), are short term or long term.

On the other hand, using a trend or longitudinal design, and focusing on the 1940 to 1980 period is fraught with possible methodological, and perhaps even conceptual disasters. The first of these, and the most bothersome is the issue of data comparability. The census data upon which analysis are based have evolved over the past 50 years in such a way that many questions in the 1980 census are not available in previous censuses. In some cases, even when the same questions were available, they were asked in different ways. For example, while it is possible to determine the percentage of the population on public assistance in 1980, 1970, and 1960, it is impossible to do so in 1950 and 1940. Similarly, an important variable, year of immigration is missing completely in all the samples of the *Demographics of Aging File*. In 1970, the variable language used at home, was not asked of 'native' English speakers. It is missing in the 1940, 1950, and 1960 samples.

In view of the above data limitations, multivariate techniques will be applied only on data from decades for which complete and comparable information is available.

The Unit of Analysis

In testing theories, it is important to relate concepts and hypotheses to their proper units of analysis. In the case of the labor market effects of immigration, the above is especially crucial. The presence of a positive relationship between immigration and earnings does not necessarily imply that immigration has beneficial effects on the labor market. It may well be that the positive effect holds for immigrants, but natives could still be adversely affected.

To minimize the risk of arriving at erroneous or fallacious conclusions, three units of analysis are used. Some hypotheses which conceptually imply individual characteristics are tested using individuals as the unit of analysis. Hypotheses that assume macro level analysis are tested at the aggregate level.

The units of study of ecological variables are Metropolitan Statistical Areas (formerly SMSAs). Unfortunately, in the *Demographics of Aging File*, only the 1980 sample can be aggregated by MSAs. For the 1940 through 1970 samples, states are used as the unit of analysis. Individuals, MSAs, and states are used when considering the 1 percent Public Use Microdata (B) Sample.

The Demographics of Aging File comprises 62,875 sampled individuals. The specific numbers are 12,656 in 1940, 12,774 in 1950, 12,018 in 1960, 12,517 in 1970, and 12,910 in 1980. A stratified sampling procedure was originally used to compile the data (ICPSR, 1987:iv). Thus, as recommended by ICPSR, to avoid biased estimates in statistical analysis, the samples above will be weighted by the respective variables provided in the code book.

Dependent Variables for Micro Level Analysis

A summary of the dependent variables (for individual level analysis), and their measurements is presented in Figure 4.1.

Earnings

The first dependent variable is earnings received in the year prior to the census. Earnings include money received for the entire year from wages, salary, commissions, bonuses or tips from all jobs reported before deductions for taxes, bonds, dues or other items (ICPSR, 1987; U.S. Bureau of the Census, 1983a). In 1940, the actual income in dollars was coded; in 1950, 1960, and 1970, the midpoint of $100 intervals was coded, and in 1980, the midpoint of $10 interval was used.

Earnings have frequently been used in previous research as indicators for studying labor market effects of immigration (Chiswick, 1984; Matta and Popp, 1988; Chiswick, 1978, 1986; Tienda, 1983; Borjas, 1982, 1986, 1987; Grossman, 1982; Johnson, 1980). Following Hauser (1980), some researchers transform the variable into logs to accommodate cases of high earners that might otherwise distort the distribution. The present study uses both logged and unlogged versions of this variable.

Socioeconomic Attainment and Occupational Prestige

A person's labor force outcomes are based not only on the earnings that are derived, but also on the prestige of jobs held. Research has shown that earnings in part depend on job prestige, and that the higher one's occupational prestige, the higher one's earnings. Structural functionalists in sociology (Davis and Moore, 1945) have argued that some jobs are more vital to societal operation than others; they require scarce talent and lengthy training. Consequently, they point out, such jobs are rewarded more than others not just in terms of earnings, but in prestige. Other things being equal, individuals will on average want to be in jobs that command high prestige and which lead to high socioeconomic attainment. Since they are important indicators of what persons receive from the labor force, the present study uses socioeconomic attainment and occupational prestige as dependent variables. Occupational prestige scores for 1960 and 1970 are derived from NORC (1980). Socioeconomic status scores for 1980 are obtained from Stevens and Cho (1985).

Industrial Sector

Dual labor market theorists argue that immigrants tend to be in secondary labor markets wherein they compete with natives and take away jobs from them. To investigate whether or not immigrants are in secondary labor markets, the variable industrial sector is used. Industrial sector is a continuum of people's position in industries. The continuum extends from the periphery (secondary) sector of the economy, to core and oligopolistic sectors (primary). Industrial sector is a continuous index measuring the degree of closeness to the primary sector of the economy. Scores on this variable are adapted from Tolbert, Horan, and Beck (1980). Through factor analysis, Tolbert, Horan, and Beck (1980) ranked industries from periphery (with lowest scores), to core and oligopoly, (with highest scores), in terms of such variables as assets, expenditure on advertising, four-firm concentration ratio, fringe benefit expenditure per worker, mean annual income of workers, mean annual political contributions, mean profit (or net income) of business units, median years employed with same firm for males, mean hours worked per week, mean weekly wage, and mean number of workers. A negative relationship between industrial sector and another variable implies tendency of the latter towards the secondary sector, and a positive relationship implies tendency or movement towards the primary sector.

Unemployment

Unemployment is a very important variable when considering the impact of immigration. Unfortunately, the U.S. Labor Department considers as unemployed only persons not currently at work, but who are actively looking for work. This is a major shortcoming, since discouraged workers not in the labor force are ignored. In view of the fact that discouraged workers are classified as not in the labor force, the present study defines as unemployed all persons that are not in the labor force. This classification includes persons not in the labor force, but who are looking for work, as well as persons that are not in the labor force. Since the sample is limited to persons aged 16 to 64, it is expected that the number of retired individuals will be small. Unemployment is treated as a dummy variable. Persons at work and persons not at work, but with a job are classified as employed, and they are given a code of 0. Those that are not at work, but who are looking for work, as well as persons not in the labor force are given a code of 1.

Labor Force Detachment

The operationalization of this variable follows Nagi's typology. Nagi (1989) proposed five forms of labor force behavior: *The Attached, The Marginal, The Seeking, The Departing,* and *The Detached.*

According to Nagi (1989:2), the Attached are persons generally employed full-time (35 hours or more) throughout the year. This group also includes people who began their first full-time employment during the Survey year, and a few professional, technical, and kindred workers who are employed more than 29, but less than 35 hours per week.

The *Marginal* group comprises: (1) persons at present having full-time employment, but who have experienced some unemployment during the year; (2) persons currently employed part-time and who had such employment during the year; (3) people temporarily laid-off, and (4) persons currently looking for work and who have been employed sometime during the year.

The *Seeking* are persons who reported that they were currently 'unemployed' or 'looking for work' and who had not been employed during the year preceding the census.

The *Departing* consists of people reporting employment during the year preceding the survey, but were not employed during the preceding year.

The *Detached* is made up of respondents that were neither employed, nor looking for work, and who reported no employment in the preceding year.

The census data are nor directly comparable with Nagi's survey data. However, the census contains enough information that permits a close approximation of Nagi's typology. Five census variables were used to create labor force detachment. The first two are: hours worked the previous week, and labor force status. For 1940, 1950, and 1980, the actual number of hours was coded, and for 1960 and 1970, the midpoint of the code range was used (ICPSR, 1987). The census labor force status variable for civilians is categorized into: (1) at work; (2) with a job, but not at work; (3) unemployed; (6) not in the labor force; (U.S. Bureau of the Census, 1983a:88). Other census variables used for creating labor force detachment are: Absent, coded: (1) yes, on layoff; (2) yes, on vacation, temporary illness, labor disputes, etc.; (3) not absent; (4) not reported; (0) not applicable. Looking for work was coded: (1) yes; (2) no; (3) not reported; (0) not applicable. Able to work was coded as follows: (1) no, already had a job; (2) no, temporarily ill; (3) no, other reasons (in school, etc.); (4) yes, could have taken a job; (5) not reported. For purposes of this study, *the Attached* are persons who reported being at work in the census, and who worked for 35 or more hours per week. For someone to be in the Attached group, his or her code on the census labor force status variable was 1, and the code for hours worked was 35 or more. *The Marginal* includes (1) persons with a job, but not at work (code 2 on labor force status), (2) those employed half-time (below 35 hours per week), and (3) those on layoff (codes 1 and 2 on the variable, Absent). *The Seeking* consists of persons who (1) were unemployed. This means that they were neither working, not having any job, and that they were (a) looking for work during the previous week, and (b), they were available to accept a job.

The census data do not provide enough information to capture Nagi's departing category, so the latter is not used in the present research. *The Detached* comprises individuals that were not in the labor force as considered by the census. Included in this category were discouraged workers who were out of work currently, but who were not looking for work, housewives, retired workers, disabled people, and those doing only incidental unpaid family work (U.S. Bureau of the Census, 1983a:k26).

For purposes of the analysis, labor force detachment is conceptualized as an ordinal variable, and it is coded as follows: (1) Attached; (2) Marginal; (3) Seeking; (4) Detached.

Public Assistance

A frequently raised, but curiously under researched immigration issue is the extent to which immigrants receive welfare income. Are immigrants more likely to receive public assistance income than the native born population? This and related questions are answered using a dependent variable called Public Assistance (or welfare). Public Assistance income includes cash receipts of payments made under the following government programs: aid to families with dependent children (AFDC), old-age assistance, general assistance, aid to the blind, and aid to the permanently and totally disabled. These payments are sometimes described as Supplementary Security Income. They are received from the Federal government, but may also come from State or local governments. In 1960, Social Security income was included in public assistance (U.S. Bureau of the Census, 1983a). The variable was created as a dummy, and coded as follows: (1) If respondent received any form of public assistance income in the year prior to the census; (0) If no public assistance was received.

Social Security

Social Security Income includes cash receipts of Social Security pensions, survivors' benefits, permanent disability insurance payments, and special benefit payments made by the Social Security Administration (under the national old-age, survivors', disability, and health insurance programs) before deductions of health insurance premiums. Medicare reimbursements are not included. Cash receipts of retirement, disability, and survivors' benefit payments made by the Federal government under the Railroad Retirement Act are also included (U.S. Bureau of the Census, 1983a:k-23). Social Security was included in public assistance income in 1960, so no separate estimates are made for that year. The variable is coded 1 if respondent received Social Security income in year prior to census, and 0 if not.

Figure 4.1 Summary and Measurement of Dependent Variables for
Individual Level Analysis

Variable	Description
Earnings	Total income in hundreds of dollars in the year prior to the census.
Socioeconomic Attainment/ Occupational Prestige	SES scores were derived from Stevens and Cho (1985), for 1980. Prestige scores for the 1970 and 1960 samples are from NORC.
Industrial Sector	A continuous index measuring individual labor market position. Scores on this index are derived from Tolbert, Horan, and Beck (1980). Through factor analysis they ranked industries from periphery (lowest) to core and oligopoly (highest) in terms of such variables as assets, expenditure on advertising, four-firm concentration ratio, fringe benefit expenditure per worker, mean annual income of workers, mean political contributions, mean profit (or net income) of business units, median years employed with same firm for males, mean hours worked per week, mean weekly wage, and mean number of workers.
Unemployment	A dummy variable; coded: Unemployed = 1; Employed = 0.
Labor Force detachment	Treated as an ordinal measure; coded: Attached = 1; Marginal = 2; Seeking = 3; Detached = 4.

Figure 4.1 Continued

| Public Assistance | A dummy variable; coded:
If respondent received public assistance income in year prior to census = 1; If respondent did not receive public assistance income = 0. |
| Social Security | A dummy variable; coded 1 = respondent is on Social Security income, and 0 = not on Social Security. |

Independent Variables for Individual Level Analysis

Education
    Education, the first independent variable is measured by years of school completed. In general, studies of immigration testing the human capital theory have stressed the role of education in maximizing returns to individuals in the labor market (Portes and Bach, 1980; Matta and Popp, 1988). Other things being equal, those with higher levels of educational attainment are more likely to have higher earnings than those with lower educational levels.

Age
    Age has also figured prominently in immigration studies testing human capital theory (Chiswick, 1984; Tienda, 1983). Age is measured in single years, but for some analysis, it will be recoded into broad age categories: 16-24 = 1; 25-34 = 2; 35-44 = 3; 45-54 = 4; 55-64 = 5.

Labor Market Experience
    According to human capital theory, a person's performance in the labor market is determined to a considerable extent by post school job (labor market) experience. This experience is measured as Age - Schooling - 5, and by the square of experience. In subtracting years of formal schooling and 5, the average age at which schooling begins in many societies, the result is an approximate proxy for the actual time that a person has been in the labor market (Beck, Horan, and Tolbert, 1978; Mincer, 1974; Stolzenberg, 1975b; Rosenzweig, 1976).

Immigrant Status
    It is coded 1 for immigrants and, 0 for native born. Immigrants are defined as those persons that were born in countries or regions outside of the United States. Persons born abroad of American parents are classified as U.S. born.

Alien Status
    The variable Alien Status is coded as follows: (1) Naturalized citizen of the United States; (0) Not a naturalized citizen. Since the census is believed to have substantial numbers of illegal aliens, and since there is no way to clearly separate legal immigrants from illegal immigrants, the foregoing variable is a crude attempt to seek some distinctions. Alien Status, is not concerned with how the respondent

originally came to the United States. It is assumed that some respondents now classified as legal immigrants might have once been illegals that subsequently adjusted their status, through for example, amnesty or other means. The variable is contaminated, to the extent that some of those that are not naturalized may not be illegal aliens. Examples include students on F-1 visas, visitors, representatives of foreign governments, and others that might have been inadvertently counted in the census.

English Proficiency

In testing human capital theory, English proficiency is especially relevant for immigrants. English is a de facto official language of the United States. In it are carried on commerce, duties of government, instruction in schools, mass media communication, business, and so on. It would seem, therefore, that a major prerequisite of one's performance in the American labor market, regardless of immigration status is the ability to comprehend and communicate adequately in English. The variable English proficiency is used as an ordinal measure to indicate the respondent's ability to understand and speak English well. It is coded as follows: (4) Native English speaker; (3) Speak English very well; (2) Speak English well; (1) Speak English not well; (0) Speak English not at all.

Language Spoken at Home

Like English proficiency, language spoken at home is relevant to one's performance in the labor market. The variable is also a crude proxy for a person's assimilation into American culture. To the extent that the major language spoken at home is foreign, then immigrants appear still strongly tied to their home culture or 'immigrant values'. Language spoken at home is coded: (1) if it not English; (0) if it is English.

Years Since Immigration

Other things equal, the longer an immigrant has been in the United States, the more he or she has acquired American values and got assimilated into American culture. Perhaps, the more the person has improved on his or her human capital through education. Chiswick (1978:899) has shown that immigrants initially earn less than the native-born, but the gap between the two narrows the longer they are in the United States. Thus, year of immigration is important in testing negative or positive impacts of immigration on the U.S. labor market. The variable year of immigration is coded as follows: (0) Born in the United States, outlying areas, or born abroad of American parents; (1) 1975-1980; (2) 1970-1974;(3) 1965-1969; (4) Before 1960-1964; (5) 1950-1959, and (6) Before 1950.

Region
If the displacement and competition theses are correct, and if the dual labor market theory is also applicable to the data analyzed here, then displacement, in the form of unemployment should be especially severe and evident in states having disproportionately large numbers of immigrants, especially illegal aliens. To further examine these issues, the variable, region is created and coded as follows: (1) Resident in a state having large numbers of immigrants. These states include California, Florida, Illinois, New Jersey, New York, and Texas. (0) Resident in any other state.

Weeks Worked per Year
Regardless of immigration or citizenship status, a persons labor force outcomes depends to a significant degree on the number of weeks worked during the year. The analysis controls for this through the continuous variable of weeks worked in the year preceding the census.

Other Variables in the Analysis

In addition to variables already described, the study uses some control variables relevant to both immigration and labor force outcomes. These include marital status, coded: (1) if not married, (0) if married; race, coded: (1) if non-white, (0) if white; sex, coded: (1) if female, (0) if male. In addition to the above, the study uses indicators of health status as control variables. These include disability which limits work, and public transportation disability. Work Disability is coded: (1) Respondent reported having disability that limits work; (0) Respondent reported having no disability or has disability that does not limit work. (1) Respondent has public transportation disability, (0) respondent has no public transportation disability. Poverty status is coded 1, if respondent is below the government's poverty line, and 0 if above it.

Figure 4.2   Definition and Description of Independent Variables
for Individual Level Analysis

Variable	Description

Human Capital Variables

Education	Measured as years of school completed.
Experience	Measured as (Age - Schooling - 5)
Experience Squared	Square of experience.
Age	Measured in years; it was recoded for some analysis.

Immigration Variables

Immigrant Status	A dummy variable coded 1, if foreign born; 0 if born in U.S., U.S. possession, or born abroad of American parents.
Alien Status	A dummy variable, coded 1 if respondent is an alien (not a naturalized citizen); 0 if respondent is a citizen, naturalized or native born.
English Proficiency	An ordinal measure, indicating respondent's ability to understand and speak English well. Native English speaker=4; Speak English very well=3; Speak English well=2; Speak English not well=1; Speak English not at all=0.
Home Language	English spoken at home=0; Speak other language at home=1.

Figure 4.2 Continued

Years Since Immigration

If person was U.S. born, coded 0 ;
Arrived 1975-1980=1;
Arrived 1970-1974=2;
Arrived 1965-1969=3;
Arrived 1960-1964=4;
Arrived 1950-1959=5;
Arrived before 1950=6.

Other Variables

Region
A dummy variable, coded:
If living in a state with large
immigrant populations, coded 1;
If living in other state, coded 0.

Weeks Worked
Number of weeks worked in year prior to
the Census.

Marital Status
Married now=0; not now married = 1.

Race
Non white=1; white=0.

Sex
Male=0; female=1.

Work Disability
Disability limits work=1;
No disability or disability does
not limit work=0.

Public Transp. Disability
/
Has public transportation disability=1;
Has no transportation disability=0.

Poverty
A dummy variable, coded 1,
if respondent is below poverty line,
and 0 if he or she is above the poverty line.

Dependent Variables for Ecological Analysis

The micro level variables above were aggregated by states and MSAs to construct variables to be used in testing hypotheses that require macro units of analysis. The dependent variables created include:

Average Earnings of Americans

To determine whether immigrants depress earnings of the native born, It is essential to separate earnings of natives from those of immigrants, and relate immigration to the former. The possibility exists that big states or big MSAs may have higher average earnings than smaller states or MSAs. This was taken into account by creating a second average earnings score which divides average earnings by the average number of employed workers in the state or MSA. Preliminary analysis revealed no significant differences in results.

Average Socioeconomic Attainment and Prestige of Americans

The close link between earnings, socioeconomic attainment, and prestige has already been alluded to elsewhere in this study. Prestige is considered one of the positive dividends that individuals obtain from being in the labor force. If immigrants can depress earnings of Americans, the question arises as to whether they could also depress their socioeconomic status or occupational prestige. This question is answered by relating immigration to the average socioeconomic level and occupational prestige of natives in the state or MSA.

Average Industrial Sector of Americans

Like earnings and prestige, position in the core or oligopolistic sector of the economy is a positive outcome that accrues to persons in the labor market. Furthermore, persons located in core or oligopolistic industries are likely to have higher earnings on average than persons in the periphery. If immigrants can have effects on earnings and prestige of natives, they may also have significant effects on American industrial sector. To understand whether this is the case, the variable industrial sector was averaged across states (1940-1980), and MSAs (1980) for the native born. Immigrants were excluded from the data before aggregation.

Native Unemployment

One of the hypothesis tested predicts that as immigration increases, Americans are likely to be displaced. A good indicator of displacement is the state or MSA native unemployment rate. American unemployment is operationalized as the percentage of native born Americans out of work. As already mentioned, the percentage unemployed includes natives that were not at work, that were looking for work, or that were not in the labor force.

Minority Unemployment

Within the United States, displacement might affect some groups more than others. Other things equal, minorities may come into greater competition with immigrants. In view of this, non-white natives are analyzed separately. Minority unemployment is computed as the percentage of non-whites that are looking for work, or that are out of the labor force. Minorities are defined as non-whites, and the two concepts are used interchangeably in this document.

Independent Variables for Ecological Analysis

Independent variables used in aggregate level analysis include the percentage of immigrants in the state or MSA, percentage of aliens (non-citizens) in the state or MSA, average number of weeks worked, average number of hours worked, average age, percentage with some college education, average educational level, percentage non-white, percentage female, percentage divorced or separated, percentage with work disability, percentage less than 25 years old, percentage with public transportation disability, and low minority skill level. The latter was computed as the percentage of native non-whites with no education, or with only less than high school education. The macro level independent variables and their descriptive statistics are shown in Appendix A. Note that only 1980 variables are shown.

Statistical Estimation

The hypotheses are evaluated using Ordinary Least Squares as the main estimator. Since some of the dependent variables at the micro level are categorical (dummy) variables, some of the hypotheses are tested employing logistic regression. The latter technique is, however, prohibitively expensive when sample sizes are large and the investigator uses several independent variables. In view of this, only sub-samples selected randomly are used in the logistic models.

Chapter 5

Descriptive Statistics

Before presenting results of the multivariate analysis on the effects of immigration on various indicators of the U.S. labor market, some basic descriptive statistics on the samples are provided. The first set of statistics presents findings on various characteristics of immigrants and native born Americans from 1940 to 1960.

Sample Characteristics, 1940 to 1960

Table 5.1 lists the characteristics of immigrants (foreign born) and Americans (natives) in 1940 through 1960. It should be said from the outset that it is difficult to apply a thorough cohort interpretation to the data. The reason is that although some immigrants in one decade definitely survived to be present in another decade, the different samples may not necessarily have the same individuals. For example, immigrants sampled in 1940 as well as natives, may not be the same as those present in subsequent samples in 1950 through 1980. A true cohort analysis assumes that the same group (comprising the same surviving individuals) is followed from one period to another (Glenn, 1977). Despite shortcomings in the data, the latter still reveal general trends that characterize immigrants and natives in the decades that are analyzed.

Table 5.1   Socio-Demographic Characteristics of Samples by Decade, 1940-1960

	1940				1950				1960			
	Immigrants		Natives		Immigrants		Natives		Immigrants		Natives	
	Number	Pct	Number	Pct	Number	Pct	Number	Pct	Number	Pct.	Number	Pct
Age												
18 - 24	142	8.6	15,891	20.0	483	5.7	14,237	17.3	1,023	11.1	12,819	14.8
25 - 34	347	20.9	20,966	26.4	927	10.9	23,082	28.1	1,689	18.3	20,455	23.6
35 - 44	503	30.3	17,597	22.1	1,483	17.4	19,538	23.8	1,794	19.4	22,078	25.5
45 - 54	359	21.7	14,990	18.9	2,756	32.4	14,715	17.9	1,767	19.1	18,716	21.6
55 - 64	307	18.5	10,043	12.6	2,866	33.7	10,486	12.8	2,950	32.1	12,492	14.4
Total	1,658	100	79,488	100	8,516	100	82,058	100	9,233	100	86,571	99.9
Race												
White	1,574	94.9	71,876	90.4	8,165	95.9	73,419	89.5	8,465	91.7	77,089	89.0
Non-White	84	5.1	7,610	9.6	351	4.1	8,639	10.5	768	8.3	9,482	11.0
Total	1,658	100	79,486	100	8,516	100	82,058	100	9,233	100	86,571	100
Sex												
Male	804	48.5	39,792	50.1	4,415	51.8	38,972	47.5	4,456	48.3	41,560	48.0
Female	854	51.5	39,696	49.9	4,101	48.2	43,086	52.5	4,776	51.7	45,011	52.0
Total	1,658	100	79,488	100	8,516	100	82,058	100	9,233	100	86,571	100

Table 5.1 Continued

	1940				1950				1960			
	Immigrants		Natives		Immigrants		Natives		Immigrants		Natives	
	Number	Pct	Number	Pct	Number	Pct	Number	Pct	Number	Pct.	Number	Pct
Marital Status												
Married	1,186	71.5	53,821	67.7	6,125	71.9	59,643	72.7	6,770	73.3	67,158	77.6
Not Married	472	28.5	25,667	32.3	2,391	28.1	22,415	27.3	2,463	26.7	19,412	22.1
Total	1,658	100	79,488	100	8,516	100	82,058	100	9,233	100	86,571	99.7
Education												
No schooling	128	7.7	1,779	2.2	625	7.3	931	1.1	390	4.0	711	0.8
Less high sch.	816	49.2	39,408	49.7	4,723	55.5	29,249	35.6	3,699	40.1	22,597	26.1
High School	590	35.6	29,242	36.8	2,264	26.6	37,977	46.3	3,626	39.3	45,128	52.1
Some College	124	7.5	8,999	11.3	905	10.6	13,901	16.9	1,518	16.4	18,133	20.9
Total	1,658	100	79,488	100	8,516	100	82,058	99.9	9,233	100	86,571	99.9

Table 5.1 Continued   Socio-Demographic Characteristics of Samples by Decade, 1940-1960

	1940				1950				1960			
	Immigrants		Natives		Immigrants		Natives		Immigrants		Natives	
	Number	Pct	Number	Pct	Number	Pct	Number	Pct	Number	Pct.	Number	Pct
Labor Force Detachment												
Attached	642	38.7	37,863	47.6	4,359	51.2	40,471	49.3	4,361	47.2	45,278	52.3
Marginal	145	8.7	5,786	7.3	682	8.0	6,388	7.8	952	10.3	8,501	9.8
Seeking	179	10.8	4,611	5.8	220	2.6	2,043	2.5	501	5.4	2,511	2.9
Detached	692	41.8	31,226	39.3	3,254	38.2	33,155	40.4	3,419	37.0	30,275	35.0
Total	1,658	100	79,488	100	8,516	100	82,058	100	9,233	99.9	86,571	100
Labor Market Experience												
None	195	11.8	4,723	5.9	835	9.8	4,613	5.6	666	7.2	4,831	5.6
1 - 10 yrs	279	16.8	19,109	24.0	428	5.0	19,057	23.2	1,311	14.2	17,931	20.7
11 - 20 yrs	143	8.6	18,065	22.7	1,202	14.1	21,250	25.9	1,725	18.7	20,696	23.9
21 - 30 yrs	452	27.2	16,311	20.5	1,430	16.8	16,267	19.8	1,464	15.9	19,201	22.2
31 - 40 yrs	364	21.9	12,884	16.2	2,009	23.6	12,757	15.5	1,734	18.8	14,436	16.7
Over 40 yrs	225	13.6	8,395	10.5	2,612	30.7	8,115	9.9	2,333	25.3	9,475	10.9
Total	1,658	99.9	79,488	99.8	8,516	100	82,058	100	9,233	100	86,571	100

Table 5.1 Continued   Socio-Demographic Characteristics of Samples by Decade, 1940-1960

	1940				1950				1960			
	Immigrants		Natives		Immigrants		Natives		Immigrants		Natives	
	Number	Pct	Number	Pct	Number	Pct	Number	Pct	Number	Pct.	Number	Pct
Hours Worked												
No Work	933	56.3	39,480	49.7	3,613	42.4	36,327	44.3	4,194	45.4	34,062	39.3
Part-time	129	7.8	4,433	5.6	544	6.4	5,260	6.4	677	7.3	7,231	8.4
Half-time	16	1.0	1,983	2.5	254	3.0	1,960	2.4	420	4.5	3,286	3.8
Full-time	580	35.0	33,592	42.3	4,105	48.2	38,512	46.9	3,941	42.7	41,992	48.5
Total	1,658	100.1	79,488	100.1	8,516	100	82,058	100	9,233	100	86,571	100
Unemployment												
Employed	787	47.4	43,649	54.9	5,041	59.2	46,860	57.1	5,313	57.5	53,782	62.1
Not	871	52.6	35,839	45.1	3,475	40.8	35,198	42.9	3,919	42.5	32,789	37.9
Total	1,658	100	79,488	100	8,516	100	82,058	100	9,233	100	86,571	100

Age

In 1940, a higher percentage of natives than immigrants were below 25 years of age. For instance, whereas 20 percent of natives in the sample were 18 to 24 years old, only 8.6% of immigrants were in the same category. In general, immigrants tended to be older than natives in 1940. With the exception of the 18 to 24 and 25 to 34 age categories, a higher percentage of immigrants than natives were in the older age categories.

The 1940 pattern with regard to age is maintained in 1950 and 1960, but with some exceptions. In 1950, like in 1940, a higher percentage of natives than immigrants were in the younger age categories (18 - 24, and 25 - 34). However, a much higher percentage of natives than immigrants were in the 35 to 44 age category (23.8 versus 17.4). Apart from this, immigrants in both the 1950 and 1960 samples were much older than natives.

Race

Among immigrants, whites predominate the racial categories. This pattern may well be a reflection of the U.S. immigration policies during this period. It will be recalled that until 1965, immigration laws favored persons from Western Europe, a region that was predominantly white.

Sex

There were very few discernible differences between immigrants and natives with regard to sexual composition. In 1940, 50.1 percent of natives were male, and a similar number (49.9) were female. Among immigrants, 48.5 percent were male, and 51.5 percent were females. In 1950, a slight reversal of the 1940 sexual composition is noted in the native category. Among natives, 47.5 percent were male, and 52.5 percent were females. Speculation suggests that this slight shift in favor of females might be an outcome of the Second World War. Since more males than females saw active combat during the 1942 through 1945 campaigns, perhaps more males died during that period. Among the foreign born (immigrants) a slightly higher percentage (51.8) were males, and 48.2 were females. A minimal difference existed among immigrants in 1960. As in 1940, 51.7 percentage of immigrant respondents were females, and 48.3 were men.

Marital Status

In 1940, a much higher percentage of immigrants (71.5) were married than that of natives (67.7). There was no major difference between the two groups in 1950. However, in 1960, higher percentage of natives were married, compared to immigrants (77.6 versus 73.3). Among both immigrants and natives, more people were married than single, divorced, or separated.

Education

In all three decades under review, a higher percentage of immigrants had no schooling when compared to the native born. In 1940, for example while only 2.2 percent of natives reported having no schooling, nearly three times this number of immigrants had no schooling. While 11.3 percent of natives had some college education, only 7.5 percent of immigrants were at a comparable level. This pattern repeated itself in 1950 and 1960. In general, the data reveal that in the period 1940 to 1960 immigrants had lower levels of educational attainment than Americans (native born).

Labor Force Detachment

In 1940, labor force detachment rates were higher among immigrants than natives. For example, while 47.6% of natives were attached to the labor force, 38.7% of immigrants were attached. About 7.3% of natives were marginal, but 8.7% of immigrants were in that category. Among natives, 5.8% sought to enter the labor force, but the number was nearly double that of immigrants, (10.8%). Among natives, 39.3% were detached from the labor force, but 41.8% of immigrants were detached. Immigrants appear to have fared much better in the 1950s than in the 1940s in terms of labor force detachment. In contrast to 1940 results, in 1950, 51.2% of immigrants were attached to the labor force, 8% were marginal, 2.6% sought to enter, and 38.2% were detached. Among the native born, 49.3% were attached, 7.8% were marginal, 2.5% were seeking to enter, and 40.4% were detached from the labor force. Rates of detachment were about equal for both foreign born and natives in 1960, except that a slightly higher percentage of immigrants was seeking to enter the labor force than natives (5.4% versus 2.9%).

Labor Market Experience

During 1940, 1950, and 1960, two extremes were observed. On the one hand, more immigrants than natives lacked labor market experience. On the other hand, however, a much larger percentage of immigrants had more than 40 years of labor market experience, compared to the native born. Differences between the two groups were especially pronounced in 1950 and 1960. In the former, 9.9% of natives had over 40 years of labor market experience. A comparable figure for immigrants was 30.7. In 1960, whereas 10.9% of the native born had over 40 years of labor market experience, 25.3% of immigrants had more than 40 years of experience.

Hours Worked per Week

In 1940, more natives worked full time than the foreign born (42.3% versus 35%). A higher percentage of the foreign born (56.3) were not at work, compared to the native born (49.7). More immigrants worked part time than natives (7.8 versus 5.6). For both immigrants and natives, work patterns were similar in 1950, although a slightly higher percentage of immigrants (48.2) worked full time than natives (46.9). The percentage of part time workers was the same for both groups (6.4).

In 1960, a much higher percentage of the native born (48.5) worked full time than immigrants (42.7). Furthermore, a higher percentage of immigrants reported not being at work than natives (45.4 versus 39.3). On the whole, the number of hours worked per week did not vary substantially among immigrants and natives in the 1940 to 1960 decades.

Unemployment

In general, results show that unemployment levels were higher among immigrants than natives in 1940 and 1960. While 52.6% of the foreign born were unemployed in 1940, 45.1% of natives were in a similar category. In 1960, 42.5% of immigrants were unemployed, but only 37.9% of natives were unemployed. Findings for 1950 show similarities among the two groups, but natives had a slightly higher percentage unemployed (42.9) than immigrants (40.8).

Sample Characteristics, 1970 to 1980

The 1970 and 1980 periods were studied separately on account of two main factors. First, U.S. immigration policies changed significantly in the late 1960s following the passage of the 1965 Amendments to the Immigration and Nationality Act. The effects of the amendments may be seen more clearly by considering the 1970 sample. In addition, most of the research controversies are associated with the nature and magnitude of immigration between 1970 and 1980. Results for the 1970 and 1980 samples are presented in Table 5.2.

Age

The age structure of immigrants and natives was similar in both 1970 and 1980. In contrast to the 1940 through 1960 decades when immigrants tended to be older than the native born, in 1970 and 1980, the immigrant population was younger.

Race

Sharp racial differences were observed in the 1970 to 1980 period, compared with earlier decades. In 1960, for example, only 8.3% of the immigrant population was non-white. In 1970, the percentage non-white had risen to 15.9, and by 1980, it stood at 35.9. This increase in the percentage of non-whites among immigrants was a result of the shift in U.S. immigration policies following 1965. It lends support to observations made in the literature that sources of immigrants have changed, with higher intakes from developing countries.

Sex

In 1970 and 1980, there were no significant differences between immigrants and natives with regard to sexual composition. Among both groups, however, females were in the majority.

Marital Status

As in prior decades, in 1970 and 1980, both natives and immigrants were more likely to be married than single, divorced or separated.

Education

The educational attainment of immigrants rose, in terms of percentage possessing some college or higher levels of schooling. In 1980, a slightly higher percentage of immigrants (39.1) than natives (38.9) had some college. On the whole, however, despite some improvements, the data reveal that immigrants continued to lag behind natives in educational attainment in the 1970 to 1980 period. It will be recalled that in 1960, 40.1% of immigrants had less than high school education. At the same time, 26.1% of natives had less than high school education. By 1970, the percentage of immigrants with less than high school education had dropped to 27.9, but it was still higher than the corresponding figure for natives (15.3). Even sharper differences between the two groups in educational attainment were noted in 1980. While only 7.4% of natives had less than high school education in 1980, nearly three times that percentage of immigrants (23) had failed to complete high school. These findings support the thesis that skill levels of immigrants have dropped. In 1970 and 1980, immigrants appeared to have much lower human capital than natives.

Labor Force Detachment

Like in 1950 and 1960, labor force detachment rates in 1970 and 1980 were higher for immigrants than natives. In 1980, for instance, more immigrants were seeking to enter the labor force than natives (5.3 versus 4.2 percent).

Labor Market Experience

The gap between immigrants and natives in the area of labor market experience noted in the 1940 to 1960 decades narrowed in 1970. By 1980, the labor market experience of both was about equal, with natives having a slight edge.

Hours Worked per Week

There were no major differences between immigrants and natives in work patterns in 1970 and 1980. In general, however, the percentage in each group working full time increased from figures observed in previous decades. In 1950, for example, 46.9% of natives worked full time, and 48.2% of immigrants worked full time. In 1980, 50.9% of natives and 48.8% of immigrants worked full time.

Unemployment

In contrast to findings for previous decades, in 1970 and 1980, among both the foreign born and native born, more persons reported being employed than unemployed. However, in 1980, immigrants had higher levels of unemployment than natives.

Table 5.2   Socio-Demographic Characteristics of Samples by Decade, 1970–1980

| | 1970 | | | | 1980 | | | |
| | Immigrants | | Natives | | Immigrants | | Natives | |
	Number	Pct	Number	Pct	Number	Pct	Number	Pct
Age								
18 - 24	2,208	19.6	18,422	18.8	2,022	19.8	25,086	20.7
25 - 34	2,339	20.7	22,602	23.1	2,657	26.0	32,728	27.0
35 - 44	2,241	19.9	20,389	20.8	2,144	21.0	23,153	19.1
45 - 54	2,412	21.4	20,302	20.7	1,788	17.5	20,722	17.1
55 - 64	2,080	18.4	16,301	16.6	1,596	15.6	19,704	16.2
Total	11,279	100.0	98,015	100.0	10,207	100.0	121,394	100.0
Race								
White	9,483	84.1	87,546	89.3	6,544	64.1	104,685	86.2
Non-White	1,796	15.9	10,468	10.7	3,662	35.9	16,709	13.8
Total	11,279	100.0	98,015	100.0	10,207	100.0	121,394	100.0
Sex								
Male	5,191	46.0	46,547	47.5	4,971	48.7	57,871	47.7
Female	6,088	54.0	51,468	52.5	5,236	51.3	63,524	52.3
Total	11,279	100.0	98,015	100.0	10,207	100.0	121,394	100.0
Marital Status								
Married	7,725	68.5	72,547	74.0	6,951	68.1	79,432	65.4
Not Married	3,553	31.5	25,467	26.0	3,255	31.9	41,962	34.6
Total	11,279	100.0	98,015	100.0	10,207	100.0	121,394	100.0
Education								
No schooling	198	1.8	873	0.9	222	2.2	510	0.4
Less high sch.	3,147	27.9	15,001	15.3	2,352	23.0	9,020	7.4
High School	5,652	50.1	55,221	56.3	3,638	35.6	64,665	53.3
Some College	2,282	20.2	26,916	27.5	3,994	39.1	47,199	39.9
Total	11,279	100.0	98,015	100.0	10,207	99.9	121,394	100.0

Table 5.2 Continued

| | 1970 | | | | 1980 | | | |
| | Immigrants | | Natives | | Immigrants | | Natives | |
	Number	Pct	Number	Pct	Number	Pct	Number	Pct
Labor Force Detachment								
Attached	5,988	53.1	52,615	53.7	5,430	53.2	67,957	56.0
Marginal	1,440	12.8	12,239	12.5	1,177	11.5	16,763	13.8
Seeking	235	2.1	2,661	2.7	543	5.3	5,140	4.2
Detached	3,617	32.1	30,499	31.1	3,056	29.9	31,534	26.0
Total	11,279	100.1	98,015	100.0	10,206	99.9	121,394	100.0
Labor Market Experience								
No Experience	916	8.1	8,625	8.8	738	7.2	10,436	8.6
1 - 10 years	2,185	19.4	24,210	24.7	3,024	29.6	37,586	31.0
11 - 20 years	2,282	20.2	18,657	19.0	2,158	21.1	24,554	20.2
21 - 30 years	2,348	20.8	18,838	19.2	1,563	15.3	18,494	15.2
31 - 40 years	2,027	18.0	17,901	18.3	1,853	18.2	19,825	16.3
Over 40 years	1,521	13.5	9,750	10.6	870	8.5	10,500	8.7
Total	11,279	100.0	98,015	100.6	10,206	99.9	121,394	100.0
Hours Worked								
Not at work	4,059	36.0	34,985	35.7	3,860	37.8	39,142	32.2
Part-time	1,212	10.7	10,413	10.6	916	9.0	14,295	11.8
Half-time	423	3.7	5,049	5.2	450	4.4	6,169	5.1
Full-time	5,585	49.5	47,567	48.5	4,980	48.8	61,788	50.9
Total	11,279	99.9	98,015	100.0	10,206	100.0	121,394	100.0
Unemployment								
Employed	7,428	65.9	64,854	66.2	6,607	64.7	84,720	69.8
Unemployed	3,851	34.1	33,161	33.8	3,599	35.3	36,674	30.2
Total	11,279	100.0	98,015	100.0	10,206	100.0	121,394	100.0

Findings Regarding Other Variables

Table 5.3 presents demographic characteristics of natives and the foreign born in the 1980 1 percent (B) sample. Comments here will be limited to variables not present in the Demographics of Aging File, except in cases of discrepancy. The total sample comprised 347,665 respondents. Out of this number, 42,435 (12.2 percent) were identified as immigrants (foreign born).

Year Last Worked

A large number of immigrants had never worked, compared to the 6.5 percent of natives that reported never having worked. The corresponding percentage was nearly doubled for immigrants at 11.7.

Language Used At Home

Not surprisingly, a larger percentage of the foreign born spoke a language other than English at home. Only 7.5% of natives spoke a foreign language at home, but 77.2% of immigrants reported speaking a different language.

Work Disability

Work disability appears to be more pronounced among natives than immigrants. For instance, 5.6% of immigrants had work disability, but 9.5% of natives had work disability. Among immigrants, 1.3% had a public transportation disability, but the figure for natives was 2%.

Public Assistance and Social Security

A higher percentage of natives (3.7) was on public assistance than immigrants (3.4). Likewise, while 5.7% of natives were on Social Security, only 3.4% of immigrants were on it.

Poverty

More immigrants were in poverty than natives. Among immigrants, 15.5% were in poverty. The corresponding percentage of persons in poverty among natives was 10.5.

Table 5.3   Demographic and Social Characteristics, 1980

	Immigrants		Natives	
	Number	Pct	Number	Pct
Age				
16 - 24	9,556	22.5	75,910	24.9
25 - 34	12,049	28.4	79,560	26.1
35 - 44	8,688	20.5	54,348	17.8
45 - 54	6,822	16.1	47,616	15.6
55 - 64	5,320	12.5	47,796	15.7
Total	42,435	100.0	305,230	100.0
Income				
Below $10,000	30,249	71.3	197,868	64.8
10,000 - 19,999	8,316	19.6	67,811	22.2
20,000 - 29,999	2,580	6.1	26,918	8.8
30,000 - 39,999	685	1.6	7,195	2.4
40,000 - 49,999	257	0.6	2,372	0.8
50,000 +	348	0.8	3,066	1.0
Total	42,435	100.0	305,230	100.0
Sex				
Male	20,262	47.7	147,301	48.3
Female	22,173	52.3	157,929	51.7
Total	42,435	100.0	305,230	100.0
Race				
White	24,773	58.4	250,014	81.9
Non White	17,662	41.6	55,216	18.1
Total	42,435	100.0	305,230	100.0
Marital Status				
Married	27,348	64.4	181,982	59.6
Not married	15,087	35.6	123,248	40.4
Total	42,435	100.0	305,230	100.0

Table 5.3 Continued.

| | Immigrants | | Natives | |
	Number	Pct	Number	Pct
Education				
No schooling	1,199	2.8	1,045	0.3
Less high School	9,985	23.5	20,378	6.7
High School	16,151	38.1	159,874	52.4
Some College	15,100	35.6	123,933	40.6
Total	42,435	100.0	305,230	100.0
Labor Market Experience				
No Experience	4,242	10.0	41,681	13.7
1 - 10 years	11,264	26.5	88,704	29.1
11 - 20 year	9,795	23.1	59,350	19.4
21 - 30 years	7,525	17.7	45,061	14.8
31 - 40 years	6,073	14.3	45,598	14.9
Over 40 years	3,536	8.3	24,836	8.2
Total	42,435	100.0	305,230	100.0
Labor Force Detachment				
Attached	22,447	52.9	160,430	52.6
Marginal	5,225	12.3	44,045	14.4
Seeking	1,217	2.9	8,856	2.9
Detached	13,546	31.9	91,899	30.1
Total	42,435	100.0	305,230	100.0
Unemployment				
Employed	27,786	65.5	205,478	34.6
Unemployed	14,649	34.5	100,183	32.8
Total	42,435	100.0	305,230	100.0
Hours Worked				
Not at work	15,546	36.6	105,478	34.6
Part-time	4,442	10.5	39,322	12.9
Half-time	1,336	3.1	10,964	3.6
Full-time	21,111	49.7	149,466	49.0
Total	42,435	99.9	305,230	100.1

Table 5.3 Continued

	Immigrants		Natives	
	Number	Pct	Number	Pct
Year Last Worked				
1980	29,116	68.6	216,277	70.9
1979	2,904	6.8	22,915	7.5
1978	974	2.3	7,083	2.3
1975 - 1977	1,208	2.8	9,990	3.3
1970 - 1974	1,716	4.0	13,724	4.5
1969 or earlier	1,557	3.7	15,363	5.0
Never worked	4,960	11.7	19,878	6.5
Total	42,435	99.9	305,230	100.0
Language Used at Home				
Use foreign language	32,746	77.2	22,780	7.5
Use only English	9,689	22.8	282,450	92.5
Total	42,435	100.0	305,230	100.0
Work Disability				
No work disability	40,057	94.4	276,292	90.5
With work disability	2,378	5.6	28,938	9.5
Total	42,435	100.0	305,230	100.0
Public Transportation Disability				
None	41,863	98.7	299,060	98.0
With pub. Trans. dis.	572	1.3	6,170	2.0
Total	42,435	100.0	305,230	100.0
Public Assistance				
No public assistance	41,004	96.6	293,966	96.3
On public assistance	1,431	3.4	11,264	3.7
Total	42,235	100.0	305,230	100.0
Social Security				
Not on Soc. Security	40,975	96.6	287,906	94.3
On Social Security	1,460	3.4	17,324	5.7
Total	42,435	100.0	305,230	100.0
Poverty Status				
Above poverty	35,873	84.5	273,266	89.5
In poverty	6,562	15.5	31,964	10.5
Total	42,435	100.0	305,230	100.0

Note: Data above are from the Public Use (B) Sample, 1980 Census.

Correlations Among Micro Level Dependent Variables

An assumption in this research is that the impacts of immigration on the economy cannot be adequately captured by one measured variable. Rather, the labor market effects of immigration will be investigated by examining various indicators, including earnings, socioeconomic attainment, occupational prestige, unemployment, and economic dependence (public assistance). Means and standard deviations of the above dependent variables are shown in Table 5.4. Note that no values are given for 1940 and 1950 for socioeconomic attainment, occupational prestige or industrial sector. Correlations between the dependent variables and immigrant status are also provided. At the individual level, immigrant status was positively related to earnings in 1940, but the two were unrelated in 1950. From 1960 to 1980, being foreign born was negatively associated with earnings, with coefficients gaining strength over the years. In 1960, the relationship between immigrant status and earnings was -.021; in 1970, it was -.030, and in 1980, it stood at -.038. Unemployment and labor market detachment were both positively related to immigrant status in 1940, but there was a change in signs of the relationship in 1950. In 1960, the relationships were again positive. In 1970, being an immigrant was unrelated to labor force detachment and unemployment. In 1980, positive associations were observed between immigrant status and labor force detachment ® = .025), and unemployment ® = .029). For the bivariate relationships between immigrant status, socioeconomic attainment and prestige, and industrial sector, the data reveal a consistent negative relationship between the former (immigrant status), and each of the dependent variables in 1960, 1970, and 1980. Intercorrelations among the dependent variables are outlined in Table 5.5. Each variable's relationship with immigrant status is also given. Of prime interest is the strong correlation between labor force detachment and unemployment, an indication that both variables may be measuring the same entity.

Table 5.4 Means and Standard Deviations of the Dependent Variables, 1940-1960

Variable	1940			1950			1960		
	Mean	Std.	r with Immigr	Mean	Std.	r with Immigr	Mean	Std.	r with Immigr
Earnings (log)	3.50	2.99	.024*	4.34	3.40	.006	5.11	3.60	-.021*
Prestige	-	-	-	-	-	-	17.92	21.03	-.095*
Sector	-	-	-	-	-	-	23.35	26.24	-.075*
Detachment	2.40	1.39	.019*	2.33	1.42	-.013*	2.22	1.38	.025*
Unemployment	0.45	0.50	.021*	0.43	0.50	-.013*	0.39	0.49	.028*

Variable	1970			1980					
	Mean	Std.	r with Immigr	Mean	Std.	r with Immigr			
Earnings (log)	8.32	1.11	-.030*	6.75	3.81	-.038*			
Prestige/SES	31.86	18.57	-.046*	31.02	21.81	-.049*			
Sector	32.59	24.21	-.125*	34.49	23.88	-.038*			
Detachment	2.11	1.34	.004	2.01	1.29	.025*			
Unemployment	0.34	0.4	.002	0.31	0.46	.029*			

Table 5.5 Correlations Among Micro Level Dependent Variables

1960

	Ear	Pre	Sec	Det	Une	Pub	Imm
Earnings	1.00						
Prestige	.30*	1.00					
Sector	.43*	.26*	1.00				
Detachment	-.71*	-.25*	-.34*	1.00			
Unemployment	-.68*	-.25*	-.32*	.97*	1.00		
Pub. Assist.	.08*	.03*	.05*	-.07*	-.06*	1.00	
Immigration	-.02*	-.09*	-.07*	.03*	.03*	.04	1.00

1970

	Ear	Pre	Sec	Det	Une	Pub	Soc	Imm
Earnings	1.00							
Prestige	.30*	1.00						
Sector	.29*	.54*	1.00					
Detachment	-.51*	-.52*	-.46*	1.00				
Unemployment	-.43*	-.52*	-.44*	.96*	1.00			
Pub. Assist.	-.08*	-.11*	-.09*	.13*	.13*	1.00		
Soc. Security	-.12*	-.12*	-.10*	.19*	.09*	.19*	1.00	
Immigration	-.03*	-.05*	-.13*	.00	.00	.01*	.00	1.00

Table 5.5 Continued

1980

	Ear	SES	Sec	Det	Une	Pub	Soc	Imm
Earnings	1.00							
SES	.48*	1.00						
Sector	.53*	.40*	1.00					
Detachment	-.72*	-.47*	-.49*	1.00				
Unemployment	-.68*	-.46*	-.46*	.95*	1.00			
Pub. Assist.	-.21*	-.16*	-.13*	.21*	.21*	1.00		
Soc. Security	-.27*	-.16*	-.14*	.27*	.26*	.08*	1.00	
Immigration	-.03*	-.05*	-.04*	.02*	.03*	.03*	-.04*	1.00

* coefficient is significant at $p < .01$. Social Security data are unavailable for 1960.

Chapter 6

The Effects of Immigration on Earnings

In this chapter, findings regarding the effects of immigration on earnings are presented. The chapter is divided into two main sections. First, the effects of immigrant status on earnings in general for the various decades under review are presented. This section reviews analysis at the micro level. To know the impact of immigration on earnings, a useful starting point is to find out about the earnings of immigrants. Individual level analysis identifies patterns of immigrant earnings from 1940 to 1980.

From a policy point of view, it is not enough to know about the earnings of immigrants. A considerable amount of inconsistencies in the literature as well as controversies in immigration discourse have centered on how immigrants affect the earnings of (native born) Americans. Individual level studies do not allow us to have an adequate understanding of the effects of immigration on the earnings of the native born. Ecological studies on the other hand can relate immigration to American earnings, with a view to unraveling whether immigrants depress the earnings of natives. In the light of this, in the second section, findings on aggregate analysis are presented. First, the impact of immigration on native earnings as a whole is analyzed. A model incorporating regional economic growth is also reviewed. Finally, separate results of the impact of immigration on minority (non-white American) earnings are outlined.

The Effect of Immigrant Status on Earnings, 1940 to 1980

The question of immigrant earnings vis-a-vis natives remains a subject of ongoing controversy. Previous studies have shown that immigrants, especially illegals earn less than natives. Interpretations as to why this is the case have ranged from immigrants' reduced human capital relative to natives, to charges that immigrants are more willing than natives to accept jobs that pay less. As a consequence, the argument goes, immigrants depress wages in the regions in which they settle. To investigate wage depression, first an attempt was made to determine whether immigrant status per se, influences earnings, and if so, the nature of the effect.

Table 6.1 prevents regression results for the effects of immigrant status on earnings in general. Results shown are for the period 1940 to 1980. This is an interesting period to look at, in that it lets us see the effects of immigration immediately before the 1965 quota restrictions were removed and new immigration patterns began. Prior to 1965, U.S. immigration laws and policies were of such a nature that in general they favored immigration from Western Europe, and either directly or indirectly, discouraged immigration from other regions of the world. Despite the passage of the 1965 Immigration and Nationality Act, immigration policies still favored Western Europeans as a consequence of the emphasis on family reunification. However, theoretically, if not in fact, it became possible for immigrants from other regions to be admitted.

Observers point out that since 1965, immigration to the United States has changed dramatically, and increasingly, more and more persons are entering from Latin America and Asia. This shift in immigrant sources has been termed as the new immigration. Since a majority of the new comers are from Third World countries, it has been argued that they have less human capital than previous comers, and in view of this they tend to have detrimental effects on the U.S. labor market. If post 1965 immigrants have had negative effects on the U.S. labor market, then we should observe differences between results for 1940 through 1960 on the one hand, and 1970 through 1980 on the other.

Proponents of human capital theory have always held that human capital variables are highly predictive of earnings. Hence in Table 6.1, the effects of immigrant status on earnings are examined while controlling for human capital and various other variables as dictated by previous research. Unless otherwise indicated, variables' effects are statistically significant at $p < .05$ if computed t-ratios are greater than 1.96.

Results in Table 6.1 show that at the individual level, even after adjusting for human capital variables (education and age), immigrant status had significant positive effects on earnings in 1940, 1950, and 1960. These effects were however, generally weak, and they were strongest in 1940. To fully appreciate their strength, it is important to examine both the partial regression (metric) coefficients and the standardized (beta) regression estimates. The former illustrates the average change in the dependent variable, (in this case log of earnings), associated with a unit change in an independent variable (in this case, immigrant status), when other variables in the equation are controlled or held constant (Berry and Feldman, 1985). The unstandardized regression coefficient for immigrant status in the 1940 equation is .755, suggesting that immigrants earned significantly more than natives in 1940 with a difference in log of earnings of .755, under the assumption that other variables remain constant. In 1950, immigrants earned slightly more on average than the native born by a difference in log earnings of .134. By 1960, although immigrants earned significantly more than natives, the difference in earnings between the two groups had narrowed to .063.

Before looking at comparable figures for 1970 and 1980, it is worth considering the standardized regression coefficients, also referred to as beta coefficients. Standardized coefficients measure the standard deviation unit change in the dependent variable that results from a standard deviation change in the independent variables. Examining the respective equations again, in 1940, a standard deviation change in immigrant status led to a .035 standard deviation change in earnings. Correspondingly, in 1950, a standard deviation change in immigration resulted into .011 standard deviation unit change in earnings. In 1960, one standard deviation change in immigrant status brought about a .005 standard deviation change in earnings. These results show that in 1940, 1950, and 1960 immigrant status did have significant and positive effects on earnings. Stated differently and more accurately, in all three decades, immigrants earned on average significantly more than the native born.

In 1970 and 1980, a noticeable and rather ominous development is the change in signs of the regression coefficients. Whereas from 1940

Table 6.1			Effects of Immigrant Status on Earnings, 1940 - 1980		
Variable	1940	1950	1960	1970	1980
Weeks Worked@					
Std. estimate	.538	.655	.741	.300	.881
t-ratio	.670	.717	.752	.550	.795
	232.481	271.964	309.462	210.600	467.229
Immigrant Status					
Std. estimate	.755	.134	.063	-.021	-.085
t-ratio	.035	.011	.005	-.006	-.006
	14.569	4.912	2.527	-2.412	-3.767
Race					
Std. estimate	-.200	-.085	.106	-.235	-.048
t-ratio	-.019	-.007	.009	-.068	-.005
	-7.790	-3.262	4.393	-27.136	-2.815
Age					
Std. estimate	.052	.019	-.024	.071	.008
t-ratio	.224	.073	-.084	.850	.030
	13.385	4.718	-5.993	46.078	2.532
Square of Age					
Std. estimate	-.000	-.000	-.000	-.000	-.000
t-ratio	-.288	-.123	-.014	-.733	-.089
	-17.376	-7.936	-.990	-39.938	-7.529
Region					
Std. estimate	.342	.241	.071	.063	.141
t-ratio	.053	.034	.010	.027	.018
	22.190	15.145	4.711	11.179	11.509
Children under 18					
Std. estimate	-.088	-.058	-.100	.000	-.009
t-ratio	-.046	-.026	-.046	.000	-.003
	-18.580	-10.851	-20.485	.185	-1.645
Marital Status					
Std. estimate	.235	.435	.069	-.137	.079
t-ratio	.037	.057	.008	-.056	.010
	13.936	24.099	3.740	-20.759	5.687

Table 6.1   Continued

Education	.069	.011	.025	.067	.058
Std. estimate	.076	.011	.024	.180	.044
t-ratio	29.294	4.495	11.007	70.524	26.481
Sex	-.442	-.345	-.297	-.533	-.339
Std. estimate	-.074	-.051	-.041	-.237	-.044
t-ratio	-25.948	-19.466	-17.273	-92.483	-27.141
R^2	.552	.574	.613	.555	.691
No. of Observations	79,237	89,019	95,803	75,305	130,868

@unstandardized estimate

to 1960 the effects of immigrant status were positive, in 1970 and 1980 they were negative. In 1970, immigrants earned on average a log earnings of .021 less than natives, and in 1980, the difference between the two groups had risen to .085. In standard deviation units, in both 1970 and 1980, a standard deviation increment in immigrant status corresponded with a .006 standard deviation decrease in earnings. Results here show that although immigrants in 1970 and 1980 earned less than natives on average, the differences between the two groups were so small that at least at the national level in the United States, they were inconsequential.

Results here, however, should not be misunderstood or misinterpreted. They do not mean, and nor do they show that in 1970 and 1980 immigrants had negative effects on the earnings of natives, the question most frequently posed in the literature. The results simply imply that being an immigrant in 1970 and 1980 on average implied having lower earnings than being an American. To determine whether Americans have been hurt by immigration with regard to their earnings, findings at the aggregate level are presented in the next section. Before that, however, results concerning other variables' effects on earnings are outlined.

Immigrants are not evenly distributed in the country; some states have higher concentrations than others. In view of this, it could be argued that perhaps the negative effects of immigration would be felt most in those states that have large numbers of immigrants. The states that have frequently been mentioned in this connection include California, Texas, Florida, New York, and Illinois. To assess the possibility of immigration having especially negative effects on these states, the dummy variable REGION was introduced into the equation. Results show that these states had on average higher earnings than others for all five decades. These results should be interpreted cautiously. They do not mean that the positive earnings were due to immigration. Indeed, it is possible that higher earnings in these states may have had the effect of drawing potential immigrants to live in them. If this interpretation is accepted, it will lend some support to equilibrium theory. Only the ecological level results presented later will illustrate whether in fact immigrants have detrimental effects on earnings of native born Americans in the states in which they settle.

Education, the most prominent of the human capital variables is consistently positively related to earnings in all five decades under

Table 6.2 The Effect of Immigrant Status on Earnings in Dollars, 1940 - 1980

Variable	1940	1950	1960	1970	1980
Weeks Worked	101.61@	240.15	382.95	702.56	1341.73
Std. estimate	.47	.53	.45	.26	.43
t-ratio	141.02	176.49	153.84	85.01	187.60
Immigrant Status	151.73	105.87	-24.33	-32.56	-.73
Std. estimate	.03	.02	-.00	-.00	-.00
t-ratio	9.39	6.87	-.94	-.63	-.01
Race	-151.14	-307.95	-469.45	-1100.89	-482.47
Std. estimate	-.05	-.05	-.05	-.06	-.02
t-ratio	-18.82	-20.87	-18.07	-21.93	-7.49
Age	29.74	60.22	127.47	377.16	641.50
Std. estimate	.48	.46	.18	.92	.81
t-ratio	24.43	25.87	31.11	42.32	51.33
Square of Age	-.33	-.64	-1.37	-3.80	-6.57
Std. estimate	-.41	-.39	-.46	-.74	-.67
t-ratio	-21.43	-22.23	-27.05	-34.11	-42.14
Region	105.44	177.60	284.75	378.14	320.48
Std. estimate	.06	.05	.04	.03	.01
t-ratio	21.95	19.76	18.07	11.61	6.89
Children under 18	-21.28	-11.65	-14.17	176.67	286.04
Std. estimate	-.04	-.01	-.01	.05	.03
t-ratio	-14.40	-3.83	-2.80	16.08	14.45
Marital Status	-116.11	-160.01	-483.75	-850.59	-1316.16
Std. estimate	-.07	-.04	-.07	-.07	-.06
t-ratio	-22.14	-15.70	-25.29	-22.28	-25.02

Table 6.2 Continued

Education	49.09	60.47	162.10	484.95	636.76
Std. estimate	.20	.12	.18	.27	.17
t-ratio	66.75	44.27	67.53	87.84	76.86
Sex	-209.89	-508.66	-1489.65	-3337.27	-5671.92
Std. estimate	-.13	-.15	-.24	-.30	-.26
t-ratio	-39.56	-50.80	-83.25	-99.99	-119.84
R^2	.39	.44	.45	.38	.44
No. of Observations	79,237	89,019	95,803	75,305	130,868

@ unstandardized estimate

review. This finding, while not surprising, adds some credence to human capital interpretations of earnings determination. Other human capital variables often used in research are labor market experience and age. It was not possible to use experience in the present analysis due to unacceptably high inter-correlations between the variable and education. Consequently, education, age, and the square of age were used as indicators of human capital. Age had positive and significant effects on earnings, except in 1960 when a negative effect was observed.

With regard to race, non-whites had lower earnings for all the decades except in 1960. In 1940, non-whites earned on average a log earnings of .200 less than whites. Corresponding figures for 1950, 1970, and 1980 are -.085, -.235 and -.048, with the most severe negative impact of race on earnings occurring in 1970. Females have consistently lower earnings than men in all the years studied. Regression coefficients are -.442 (1940); -.345 (1950); -.297 (1960); -.533 (1970), and -.339 (1980).

Comparing the relative effects of the various variables on earnings, the standardized regression estimates (beta weights) show that the most important determinant of earnings is the number of weeks the individual worked. Next in the order of influence is age. The respective equations explained 55 percent of the variation in earnings in 1940; 57 percent in 1950; 61 percent in 1960; nearly 56 percent in 1970, and 69 percent in 1980.

The equations in Table 6.1 were re-estimated, using the unlogged version of the dependent variable. One advantage of using earnings unlogged is that interpreting the results becomes much clearer and easier.

Table 6.2 presents results of micro level determinants of earnings, with the dependent variable unlogged. A number of interesting results emerge. When the logged form of earnings was used previously (Table 6.1), immigrant status had positive effects on earnings from 1940 to 1960. Then negative effects were seen in 1970 and 1980. In the unlogged specification of the dependent variable in Table 6.2, immigrants had higher earnings than natives in only 1940 and 1950. From 1960 to 1980, immigrants did not earn significantly less than natives. Results as a whole are more consistent across different decades when the unlogged version of earnings is used. For example, age is now positively related to earnings across the various time periods. This is in contrast to findings in Table 6.1 when curiously enough, age had negative effects on earnings in 1960.

Another anomalous finding in the logged specification of earnings that seems to have been corrected by the unlogged version has to do with marital status. In Table 6.1, marital status (being divorced, separated, single, or widowed) had positive effects on earnings in 1940, 1950, 1960, and 1980. When earnings are unlogged (Table 6.2), unmarried persons earn significantly less than the married in all time panels. Race (being non-white) also has significant negative impacts on earnings for all the years. On average, non-whites made $151.14 less than whites in 1940. By 1970, they were making on average $1,100.89 less than whites, and in 1980, non-whites made $482.47 less than whites. Previously (Table 6.1), race had a positive effect on earnings in 1960. As before, females have significant and consistently lower earnings than men in all decades. Additionally, the coefficients (both standardized and unstandardized) appear to increase over time, perhaps supporting the contention that the income gap between the sexes did not narrow between 1940 and 1980. In 1940, females made $209.89 less than men. In 1960, they made $1,489.65 less than men, and by 1980, they were making on average $5,671.92 less than men.

The discrepancies observed between results in Tables 6.1 and 6.2 suggest that earnings as a dependent variable is very sensitive to its functional specification. Since different results are obtained for key variables depending on whether earnings is unlogged or not, it may well be that studies that have relied on only the logged form and found immigrant status negatively related to earnings in 1970 and 1980 may have derived erroneous conclusions. By changing the dependent variable into elasticities through log transformation, researchers improve on the explanatory power of their equations or models. A comparison of Tables 6.1 and 6.2 reveal that the logged version of income provides higher coefficients of determination than the unlogged equations. However, given the controversial nature of the entire immigration issue, it is probably more appropriate that focus be shifted from maximizing R^2s to examining the strength and directions of individual coefficients. It appears at this point that specifying earnings unlogged is a sound way to begin to do this, except in cases where severe skewness is found.

A noticeable flaw in the equations in Table 6.1 is that some potentially relevant variables have been omitted. It is possible, for example, that the negative effects of immigrant status on earnings might disappear if we control for number of years since immigration, and language proficiency. It is also necessary to control for health related variables. Since the Demographics of Aging File upon which Table 6.1 is based does not contain information on the foregoing variables, data on the 1 percent (B) sample from the 1980 Census were used to estimate the effects of the variables in Table 6.1, while controlling for the effects of the additional variables. The census does not contain information on health, but it has a variable that could be used as proxy. This is work disability. Results of the expanded model are shown in Table 6.3. Note that the dependent variable is given in its logged form to make comparisons possible with findings in Table 6.1. The unlogged equivalent is given in Table 6.4.

Findings reported in Table 6.3 show that when the dependent variable is logged, immigration is still negatively related to earnings. However, years since immigration has a slight positive effect on earnings, with a metric coefficient of .003, a standardized estimate of .003, and a t-ratio of 2.113. These findings suggest that in general, immigrants may have lower earnings, but their earnings increase the longer they are in the United States. Results also indicate that lack of proficiency in the English language leads to lower earnings. Work disability emerges in the new model as one of the most important predictors of earnings. Its unstandardized regression coefficient is -.352, and the standardized coefficient is -.024, both indicating that work disability reduces one's earnings.

A frequently discussed issue is that although immigrants as a whole may have only minor negative effects on the U.S. labor market, illegal immigrants have significant detrimental impacts. Unfortunately, there is no direct way of assessing the effects of illegal aliens from the census. However, the 1980 census asked respondents to indicate whether or not they were citizens of the United States. From this question, it is possible to derive a proxy for illegal aliens. Illegal aliens are generally reluctant to come into contact with government officials for fear of being caught, and in view of this, few, if any would respond to census questionnaires. Despite this, however, there have been numerous reports that lots of illegal aliens were indeed counted in the 1980 census. Thus, although data based on citizenship may not capture illegal aliens, it is the only best thing.

There are thousands of people in the United States that are not citizens, but at the same time, they are not illegal aliens. Examples include visitors, students, exchange scholars, and representatives of

Table 6.3 The Effect of Immigrant Status on Earnings, 1980

Independent Variable	b	Beta	t-ratio	Prob.
Weeks Worked in 1979	.146	.781	679.419	.000
Immigrant Status	-.143	-.011	-5.866	.000
Race	-.033	-.003	-3.084	.001
Age	.010	.033	4.478	.000
Square of Age	-.000	-.032	-4.350	.000
Region	-.000	-.000	-.091	.485
Children under 18	-.005	-.002	-1.548	.061
Marital Status	-.178	-.021	-17.010	.000
Education	.051	.040	35.929	.000
Sex	-.213	-.026	-24.260	.000
Work Disability	-.352	-.024	-22.482	.000
Years Since Immigration	.003	.003	2.113	.018
English Proficiency	.052	.009	6.697	.000
R^2		.649		
Number of Observations		347,665		

foreign governments. It is conceivable that the variable captures the effects of some of these people if they happen to have responded to the census questionnaires. It is important to note, however, that the line between illegal aliens and immigrants is very thin. Indeed, some of the people who claimed to be naturalized citizens might have at one point been illegal aliens themselves. Some may not be citizens, but may consider themselves so once they have filed their applications for citizenship, even before the process is completed. In view of these difficulties, the variable Alien Status was used only as a proxy for illegals.

The census has not been consistent with regard to the question on citizenship. In 1980, it was asked of all respondents, but in 1970, it was asked only of the foreign born. It is absent in the Demographics of Aging File for all the years, except 1980. Consequently, analysis on aliens are limited to 1980. Alien Status was highly related to immigrant status, with a correlation coefficient of .735. Such a high coefficient only highlights the problem already raised that the line between who is an immigrant and who is an alien is often not clear. Conceivably, problems of multicollinearity might arise if both variables are used in a regression equation. However, with such a large sample, and given the level of analysis, multicollinearty is not a serious concern.

Alien Status was substituted for immigrant status in the equation in Table 6.3. There was no change in explained variance. The R^2 remained at .649. Analysis (not presented) showed that aliens have significantly lower earnings than citizens. The unstandardized coefficient for the effects of aliens was -.102, the standardized estimate was -.006, and the t-ratio was -4.683. Year of immigration was negative, but unrelated to earnings in the new equation. Other effects remained as on Table 6.3.

Table 6.4 gives findings with earnings unlogged. The proxy for illegal aliens (Alien status) is also included in the model. Results show no strong relationship between immigrant status and earnings when Alien Status is controlled. However, aliens (non-citizens) have significantly lower earnings than citizens. On average, non-citizens earn $377.13 less than citizens. For both aliens and immigrants, earnings increase as years of residence in the United States increase. Each additional year of residence in the United States increases earnings by an average of $9.61. English proficiency was unrelated to earnings.

Table 6.4

Micro Level Determinants of Earnings in Dollars, 1980

Independent Variable	b	Beta	t-ratio	Prob.
Immigrant Status	-144.92	-.004	-1.438	.075
Alien Status	-377.13	-.009	-4.198	.000
Years Since Immigration	9.61	.005	2.223	.013
Weeks Worked in 1979	213.22	.432	291.789	.000
Sex	-4660.12	-.213	-155.785	.000
Race	-350.42	-.013	-9.532	.000
Education	532.83	.158	110.373	.000
Marital Status	-1217.00	-.054	-34.301	.000
Work Disability	-1528.53	-.040	-28.738	.000
Children under 18	-171.18	-.022	-15.525	.000
Age	464.04	.592	62.356	.000
Square of Age	-4.54	-.457	-48.771	.000
English Proficiency	41.83	.003	1.537	.062
Region	292.79	.013	9.832	.000
R^2		.417		
Number of Observations		347,665		

Work disability remained a strong hindrance to earnings. Persons with disability earned on average $1,528.53 less than those without disability. Gender also remained a major obstacle to higher earnings, with females on average earning $4,660.12 less than males. Non-whites continued having lower earnings than whites, with a difference of $350.42 between the two groups. Single, divorced, and separated individuals earned considerably less than married individuals. The former earned on average $1,217.00 less than the married in 1980. The human capital variables, education and age, together with weeks worked were the strongest determinants of earnings.

Effects of Immigration on Native Earnings, 1940 to 1980

The question of whether immigration benefits or hurts the United States cannot be fully addressed without examining the impact that immigrants have on the earnings of native born citizens. Unresolved questions remain concerning whether or not immigrants depress American earnings. Sound immigration policy regarding this issue cannot be determined until it has been fully investigated and empirical and definitive results are obtained. This section presents analysis of the effects of immigration on American earnings.

American (native) earnings were specified in actual dollars. Log transformations were done, but results were identical. Furthermore, the skewness (1.532) was negligible to warrant maintaining log transformation. Thus, to make interpretations easy, it was decided to stick to dollar amounts. All variables were aggregated by states. Additional results are presented on aggregation by MSAs. Variables in the analysis include: percentage of immigrants in the state, percentage females, percentage with college education, average number of weeks worked, and average age. State average educational attainment was substituted for percentage with college education, but with negligible difference in results. Percentage divorced or separated was also included in the equation, but it made no significant contribution. Consequently, to maximize scarce degrees of freedom in the face of a small sample size, and also in the interest of parsimony, only five independent variables are included in the analysis.

Results of the analysis of the consequences of immigration on native earnings are presented in Table 6.5. Findings indicate that for every decade in the panels, except 1940, immigration had significant positive

Table 6.5

Effects of Immigration on Native Earnings in Dollars, 1940 - 1980

Variable	1940	1950	1960	1970	1980
Pct. Immigrants	-4.363[@]	23.900[a]	52.992[a]	54.998[a]	126.388[a]
Std. estimate	-.141	.330	.397	.383	.277
t-ratio	-.955	2.634	3.093	2.917	2.343
Pct. College Educat.	8.487[b]	9.844[b]	-32.392[a]	19.017[c]	98.267[a]
Std. estimate	.271	.231	-.330	.214	.563
t-ratio	2.124	1.996	-2.461	1.568	4.615
Pct. Female	-8.844[a]	-15.260[b]	-54.682[a]	-4.226	-153.597[b]
Std. estimate	-.479	-.296	-.335	-.012	-.247
t-ratio	-3.247	-1.790	-2.516	-.073	-2.091
Average Age	6.442	-41.782[c]	38.780	-53.065	-28.504
Std. estimate	.097	-.189	.056	-.086	-.016
t-ratio	.721	-1.496	.424	-.516	-.116
Ave. Weeks Worked	23.094	173.109[b]	70.251[b]	86.665[b]	125.096[c]
Std. estimate	.090	.305	.227	.257	.162
t-ratio	.629	1.855	1.735	1.831	1.471
R^2	.331	.496	.316	.292	.495
Adj. R^2	.253	.437	.240	.213	.439
Number of Observations	49	49	51	51	51

a significant at p < .01. (one-tailed test).
b significant at p < .05. (one-tailed test).
c significant at p < .10. (one-tailed test).
@ unstandardized estimate

effects on native earnings. In the 1950, a one-percentage increase in immigration was associated with an increase of \$23.90 in native earnings. In 1960, on average a one-percent increase in immigration led to a \$52.99 increase in native earnings. A one-percent increase in immigration in 1970 raised native earnings by nearly \$55.00, and in 1980, a one-percent increase in immigration brought about a corresponding increase in native earnings of \$126.39.

These results seem to suggest that immigrants as a group do not depress American earnings as some past studies have found. It appears that immigrants make positive contributions to American earnings, implying that immigration might not have hurt the United States. The sign of the relationship between immigration and native earnings is negative in 1940. This represents a paradox. At the individual level, it was found that in 1940, immigrants earned significantly more than Americans. How explain the fact that they seem to have depressed American earnings at that time?

Two possibilities may account for this. One is that the 1930 to 1940 decade captured by   findings in 1940 was a period of the Great Depression. Immigration was at an all time low in that decade. In fact, it has been observed that even illegal immigration from Mexico came to a   virtual halt in the Depression.   The insignificant and negative coefficient may in part, be a function of economic stagnation. Second, Adolf Hitler's increasing bellicose attitude and early victories probably led to the departure from some European nations (and Germany itself) of people that were highly educated, and thus, had high levels of human capital. It may, therefore, be that competition from pre-1940 immigrants to the United States was directed at Americans at the higher levels of the occupational spectrum.

Results in Table 6.5 show that college education has significant effects on earnings. However, returns to education were negative in 1960. In 1970, college education made no significant contribution to native earnings. Education appears to have made the highest returns to earnings in 1980. Females had significant depressing effects on earnings across all time panels, except in 1970 when no effect was found. The negative effect is captured most in the decade of the Depression, 1930 to 1940 (evident in the 1940 panel).

Although immigrants do not seem to depress American earnings at the national level, it is conceivable that in regions with above average concentrations, immigrants could have adverse effects. To investigate this possibility, states with 5% or more of immigrants were analyzed separately. In 1940, due to the small percent of immigrants in the country, 1% was used as the cutoff point. Results of the analysis on immigrant enclaves are presented in Appendix B.

Findings in Appendix B show that in immigrant enclaves, immigration still has some positive effects on native earnings, but with two exceptions. In 1940, immigrants had negative impacts on American earnings. The regression coefficient of -19.248 illustrate that in 1940, on average for every one percent increase in immigration in states that already had over 1 percent or more immigrants, there was a corresponding decrease of $19.25 in native earnings. These negative findings in 1940 may once again reflect the unique political and economic situation during that period. The Great Depression, coupled with the Second World War meant that natives had fewer resources. As a result, increases in immigration only made competition for scarce resources even more stringent. In 1950, 1960, and 1970, immigrants continued to make positive contributions to the earnings of natives, but their contributions weakened with time. In 1980, there was no significant impact of immigration on earnings.

Results reveal that females still negatively influenced earnings. In sharp contrast to previous findings, in 1970, females made a significant positive contribution to native earnings. In fact in the 1970 equation, the variable percentage female is the strongest determinant of native earnings. The positive influence observed during that period may well be a reflection of increased female labor force participation in the 1960 to 1970 decade. A possible impact of the Women's Movement should not be underestimated or discounted.

Effects of Immigration on Native Earnings
Controlling for Economic Expansion, 1940 to 1980

Equilibrium theorists hold that population movement is due to regional economic imbalances. Implicit in this assertion is that workers move from areas of low wage rates to regions with higher wages. The foregoing statements lead to the proposition that states with higher wage rates will tend to attract more people to move into them. Conceivably, states with higher wage rates have experienced greater economic growth than others. Other things equal, the higher the rate of economic expansion, the higher the level of earnings in a given state.

Past studies have found that immigrants are not evenly distributed in the United States; only a few states appear to be chosen as immigrant destinations and places of settlement. Although it has been found that immigration has positive effects on American earnings, an important question remains to be answered: Are these positive effects due to immigration per se, or are they brought about by general regional growth dynamics? Put differently, could the observed positive effects of immigration on American earnings be spurious?

To examine the issue of spuriousness, the equations in Table 6.5 were re-estimated, while controlling for the effects of regional economic growth. The variable economic expansion was created as a dummy. States that had earnings above the national average in the year prior to the census were given a code of 1. States below the national average were given a code of 0. Average state earnings were: $445.37 (in 1940), $1,149.77 (in 1950), $2,274.46 (in 1960), $4,056.41 (in 1970), and $9,100.89 (in 1980).

Relevant extracts of the regression analysis incorporating economic expansion are presented in Table 6.6. Results show that in each decade studied, American earnings were significantly a function of regional growth patterns. States above the national earnings average (states that had experienced economic expansion) had significantly higher earnings than states that had experienced lower growth. The sharpest disparity was found in the 1930 to 1940 decade, as reflected in the 1940 panel.

Results in Table 6.6 show that even after controlling for economic expansion (regional disparities), immigration continued to have significant effects on American earnings. All the directions were positive, except in 1940 when the coefficients not only remained negative, but became statistically significant. In that year, a 1% increase in immigration reduced American earnings on average by $7. Possible reasons for the negative impact of immigration on earnings have already been given. The economic problems created by the Depression of the late 1920s and 1930s meant fewer jobs and opportunities. This in turn led to reduced immigration from Mexico of low level manpower. At the same time, the Depression had hardly ended by the outbreak of hostilities in Europe in the late 1930s. The latter brought about sharp increases in immigration of higher level manpower from European countries. Competition from the new entrants from Europe would have been directed at Americans with higher or comparable skills as the new comers. In the face of reduced economic opportunities and slow growth, such a competition led to lower American earnings.

If the above analysis is accurate, then it follows that the effects of immigration on American society depend largely on the nation's

Table 6.6   Effects of Immigration and Economic Expansion on Native Earnings in Dollars, 1940 - 1980

Independent Variable	1940	1950	1960	1970	1980
Pct. Immigrants	-7.035[a]	23.891[a]	37.845[a]	31.936[b]	73.932[b]
Std. estimate	-.227	.330	.284	.218	.162
t-ratio	-2.492	3.116	2.859	2.085	1.795
Economic Expansion	299.303[a]	926.435[a]	1478.454[a]	1598.193[a]	2893.141[a]
Std. estimate	.717	.443	.599	.575	.559
t-ratio	8.486	4.272	5.861	5.730	6.065
Pct. College Educat.	3.436[c]	7.879[b]	-30.569[a]	16.882[b]	54.046[a]
Std. estimate	.110	.185	-.312	.186	.310
t-ratio	1.361	1.879	-3.064	1.771	3.091
Pct. Female	-4.405[a]	-12.373[c]	-23.931[c]	-35.470	-158.693[a]
Std. estimate	-.238	-.240	-.147	-.098	-.255
t-ratio	-2.513	-1.711	-1.384	-.778	-2.895
Average Age	9.155[b]	-9.622	-11.293	-9.073	-76.161
Std. estimate	.138	-.044	-.016	-.014	-.043
t-ratio	1.667	-.389	-.162	-.112	-.413
Ave. Weeks Worked	26.792	123.115[c]	41.091[c]	75.872[b]	75.215
Std. estimate	.104	.217	.133	.220	.097
t-ratio	1.187	1.545	1.322	2.039	1.175
R^2	.754	.649	.616	.591	.725
Adj. R^2	.718	.598	.563	.536	.687
Number of Observations	49	49	51	51	51

a significant at p < .01. (one-tailed test).
b significant at p < .05. (one-tailed test).
c significant at p < .10. (one-tailed test).
@ unstandardized estimate.

economic health. During periods of economic stagnation, immigration, even of highly skilled persons, can depress American earnings. In periods of prosperity, immigration leads to increases in native earnings.

In all the other panels, immigrants appear to have made significant and positive contributions to American earnings, but these effects weakened from their highest levels in 1950 (as reflected in the standardized estimates), to their lowest levels in 1980. In the 1950 panel, a standard deviation increment in immigration brought about a 33% standard deviation change in native earnings. Comparable figures were 28%, 22%, and 16% in 1960, 1970, and 1980 respectively. The relatively weak effect in 1980 adds some support to the economic stagnation thesis. The 1970 to 1980 period (captured in the 1980 panel), was a decade that witnessed such economic hardships as high inflation, recessions, and the energy crisis brought about in part by the Arab oil embargo. Thus, although immigrants made positive contributions to overall native earnings, their effects were small, relative to prior decades.

To further explore the issue of spuriousness, an additional analysis undertaken was to look at growth (change) in the dependent variable (native earnings) over time. Analysis was limited to the 1970 and 1980 panels. If immigration depresses native earnings, then we should observe a decrease in native earnings over time as immigration increases during the same time frame, ceteris paribus.

Relevant regression results of the effects of change in immigration on growth in native earnings are presented in Table 6.7. Findings show that increases in immigration during the 1970 to 1980 period contributed to higher earnings for Americans. A 1 percentage change in immigration brought about an increase in American (native) earnings of $108.89, adjusting for other variables in the equation in Table 6.7.

Metropolitan Level Results of the Impact of Immigration on Native Earnings, 1980

The model estimated with states as the unit of analysis was estimated at the MSA level. Percentage with work disability was added to the equation. Results of the analysis for 76 largest MSAs are presented in Table 6.8. Results show that in the decade preceding the 1980 census, immigrants did not depress native earnings. In fact, results suggest that they made positive contributions to native earnings. Findings in Table 6.8 indicate that a 1 percentage increase in immigration was associated with an increase of nearly $29.24 in native

Table 6.7   Effects of Change in Immigration on Growth in Native Earnings, 1970 - 1980

Independent Variable	b	Beta	t-ratio	Prob.
Change in Pct. Immigrants	108.89	.229[b]	1.854	.0352
Change in Weeks Worked	86.30	.152	1.220	.1145
Change in Pct. Divorced	47.50	.185[c]	1.585	.0601
Change in Pct. College Educ.	44.38	.279[a]	2.180	.0173
Change in Pct. Female	-43.81	-.106	-0.685	.2484
Change in Average Age	-402.22	-.383[a]	-2.260	.0144
R^2		.461		
Adj. R^2		.387		
Number of Observations		51		

earnings, taking into account other variables in the equation. The only novel finding is the effect of work disability. With Other variables controlled, a 1% increase in work disability in 1980 reduced native earnings by $406.56. In fact, work disability was the most important predictor of native earnings.

The equations in Table 6.8 were estimated on data for metropolitan areas with immigrant populations of 10 percent or more. Results of the analysis are shown in Appendix C. Results indicate that immigration had no significant effect on native earnings, although coefficients are still in the positive direction. The strongest predictors of native earnings now appear to be work disability (beta=-.578); college education (beta=.376); average age (beta=.363), and percentage female (beta=-.262).

The findings in Appendix C imply that in immigrant enclaves within urban areas, positive effects of immigration are absent. The net benefits of immigration on the native born appear to hold only in regions that do not have large concentrations of immigrants.

Effects of Immigration on Minority Earnings, 1980

Findings on the impact of immigration on minority earnings are given on Table 6.9. Results indicate that although immigrants do not depress earnings of the native population as a whole, they do affect the earnings of subgroups within the population. Minority earnings are significantly affected by immigrants. In Table 6.9, it is shown that a 1 standard deviation increase in immigration brought about a 39% standard deviation decrease in minority earnings. In unstandardized units, a 1% increase in immigration led to a decrease in minority earnings of nearly $25.32 on average in 1980. The t-statistic is -3.102, a significant finding at the 99% level of confidence. These findings remain even after adjusting for the effects of minority skill levels. Suggested here is that non-whites may be hurt by increases in immigration. Note that for the above analysis, only minorities (non-whites) and immigrants were aggregated by MSAs.

Table 6.8   Effects of Immigration on Native Earnings, Metropolitan Level Analysis, 1980

Variables	Earnings in Dollars	Log of Earnings
Percent Immigrants		
Std. estimate	29.336[c]	.004[b]
t-value	.118	.155
	1.519	2.114
Average Weeks Worked		
Std. estimate	205.034[b]	.028[a]
t-value	.242	.302
	1.993	2.642
Average Age		
Std. estimate	239.650[a]	.021[b]
t-value	.201	.163
	2.613	2.256
Percent College Educated		
Std. estimate	19.295	.002
t-value	.098	.082
	.997	.884
Percent Females		
Std. estimate	12.389	.000
t-value	.010	.004
	.137	.057
Percent with Work Disability		
Std. estimate	-406.556[a]	-.040[a]
t-value	-.531	-.484
	-3.597	-3.477
R^2	.684	.719
Adj. R^2	.656	.694
Number of Observations	76	76

a significant at $p < .01$ (one-tailed test).
b significant at $p < .05$ (one-tailed test).
c significant at $p < .10$ (one-tailed test).

Table 6.9   Effects of Immigration on Minority Earnings, 1980

Independent Variable	b	Beta	t-ratio	Prob.
Pct. Immigrants	-25.317	-.350	-3.102	.001
Pct. College Educated	15.818	.095	1.212	.114
Pct. Female	-69.586	-.185	-2.850	.003
Average Age	187.886	.224	3.142	.001
Pct. Divorced Minorities	-65.896	-.327	-4.646	.000
Pct. with Work Disability	-127.415	-.245	-2.905	.002
Average Weeks Worked	203.289	.428	5.152	.000
Pct. Unskilled Minorities	-104.489	-.393	-3.506	.000
R^2		.755		
Adj. R^2		.726		
Number of Observations		76		

Other findings to note include the fact that divorce among minorities is a deterrent to higher earnings. A 1% increase in divorce decreases minority earnings by $65.89. This indicates that family breakdown may be one of the main reasons for low labor market benefits derived by minorities. Work disability is also strongly tied to low minority earnings. A 1% increase in work disability depresses minority earnings by $127.42. Lack of skills among minorities is tied to low earnings, with the former lowering earnings by $104.49. The significant variables in the minority earnings equation explained nearly 76% of the variance.

Chapter 7

The Effects of Immigration on Socioeconomic Attainment and Occupational Prestige

Earnings represent just one factor that offers benefits to workers in the labor market. Occupational prestige and socioeconomic status are also very important. Research has consistently shown that occupational prestige itself is strongly tied to earnings, and that the higher the prestige of one's occupation, the higher the income. The higher one's income, the higher one's socioeconomic status and vice versa. Furthermore, past literature has found that those in high prestigious jobs, and who work under less supervision have lower levels of alienation, and report higher job satisfaction than persons who work under close supervision. In the light of all the above, it is important to determine the extent to which immigrants influence occupational prestige in the United States. Do immigrants, for example go into occupations with lower prestige than natives? Do immigrants affect the occupational prestige and socioeconomic attainment of natives? This chapter presents findings on the effects of immigrant status and immigration on socioeconomic attainment (1980) and occupational prestige (1960 and 1970).

Like the previous chapter, the current one is divided into two main sections. First, individual level findings are discussed. Analysis are limited to only 1960, 1970, and 1980. The reason for this limitation is that socioeconomic and occupational prestige scores are unavailable for 1940 and 1950. Second, aggregate (macro) level results are presented. Also as before, results using the 1 percent 1980 B sample are given.

Effects of Immigrant Status on Socioeconomic
Attainment and Occupational Prestige, 1960 to 1980

Micro level results of the effects of immigrant status on occupational prestige are shown in Table 7.1. Immigrants on average held less prestigious jobs than natives in 1960. Negative signs held in 1970, but that year immigrant status had no significant impact on prestige. In 1980, some immigrants apparently began to go into jobs with higher socioeconomic status. Their effects as evidenced by the regression coefficients is, however, too small as to warrant any useful discussion. The difference between immigrants and natives in SES in 1980 was .92 in favor of immigrants.

Non-whites were consistently in less prestigious jobs in both 1970 and 1980. Marital status affects one's SES and occupational prestige. The standardized regression coefficients are -.04, -.10, and -.03 for 1960, 1970, and 1980 respectively. Presumably, single, divorced, separated, and widowed individuals tend to be in low prestige and low SES jobs, compared to those that are currently married. Educational attainment emerged as the single most important predictor of one's occupational prestige and SES. The standardized regression coefficients were .28, .53, and .45 for 1960, 1970, and 1980 respectively. This is hardly a surprising finding. The higher one's education, the higher one's human capital, and consequently the higher the rewards bestowed on that person by society in the form of higher prestige and SES.

On, average women tended to have lower socioeconomic attainment than men in 1980. Women, however, appear to be in jobs with slightly higher prestige than men. Results in 1960 and 1970 are consistent with past research findings that women's occupational prestige scores are equal to, or in some cases greater than those of men (U.S. Commission on Civil Rights, 1978). Explanations for this have looked at the nominally higher prestige of so-called 'pink-collar' jobs, such as nursing, teaching, and clerical work. Women tend to be over represented in these occupations (Sullivan, 1984).

Some key variables were not controlled in Table 7.1, since they are absent in the *Demographics of Aging File*. To take those variables' effects into account, the model in Table 7.1 was re-estimated controlling for years since immigration, work disability, aliens, and proficiency in the English language. Findings of the analysis incorporating additional variables are shown in Table 7.2.

Table 7.1   Effects of Immigrant Status on Prestige (1960-1970), and on Socioeconomic Status (1980)

Independent Variable	Occupational Prestige						SES 1980		
	1960			1970					
	b	Beta	t	b	Beta	t	b	Beta	t
Weeks worked	1.61	.28	80.2	.83	.12	38.5	2.32	.38	170.3
Immigrant Status	-4.12	-.06	-19.7	-.19	-.00	-1.4	.92	.01	5.5
Race	-3.90	-.06	-19.0	-3.39	-.08	-25.4	-1.22	-.02	-9.8
Age	-.07	-.04	-12.8	.07	.07	20.0	.11	.07	31.8
Region	1.21	.03	9.4	.45	.02	5.3	.78	.02	8.6
Children	-.54	-.04	-11.5	-.16	-.02	-5.7	.11	.01	2.9
Marital status	-1.93	-.04	-11.4	-3.00	-.10	-30.5	-.93	-.02	-9.3
Education	1.72	.28	87.9	2.44	.53	166.3	3.30	.46	208.3
Sex	2.29	.05	15.7	.51	.02	5.8	-1.58	-.04	-17.3
R^2		.18			.31			.44	
N		95,803			75,305			130,868	

Table 7.2   The Effect of Immigrant Status on SES, 1980

Independent Variable	b	Beta	t-ratio	Prob.
Weeks Worked	.389	.393	266.94	.000
Immigrant Status	.559	.008	2.78	.005
Alien Status	-.239	-.003	-1.33	.183
Race	-2.698	-.050	-36.84	.000
Age	.567	.361	38.26	.000
Region	.366	.008	6.17	.000
Children under 18	-.416	-.027	-18.94	.000
Marital Status	-.946	-.021	-13.39	.000
Education	2.749	.407	285.87	.000
Sex	-.984	-.022	-16.50	.000
Work Disability	-.732	-.010	-6.90	.000
Years Since Immigration	-.032	-.008	-3.60	.000
English Proficiency	-.403	-.014	-7.42	.000
R^2		.424		
Number of Observations		347,665		

Immigrant status had a significant positive influence on socioeconomic attainment, implying that immigrants on average tended to have higher SES than Americans in 1980. According to the data, immigrant socioeconomic attainment decreases the longer they are in the United States. Suggested is that over time, immigrants tend to become like natives. Non-whites had lower SES than whites in 1980. Socioeconomic attainment appears to increase with age.

Divorced, single, and separated individuals have lower levels of socioeconomic attainment than the married. Persons with work disability have significantly lower SES than those without. Educational attainment was the most important predictor of an individual's socioeconomic status in 1980.

Effects of Immigration on Native Socioeconomic Attainment and occupational prestige, 1960 to 1980

In chapter 6, it was found that immigrants do not depress American earnings, and that they make positive contributions to native earnings. Although earnings are closely associated with prestige and SES, however, they are not necessarily the same. Thus, it is possible that although immigrants make positive contributions to native earnings, they may adversely affect the prestige of jobs which natives hold. Individual level analysis presented above cannot determine the degree to which immigration might influence native prestige or SES. Analysis in this section are undertaken to help unravel possible influences that immigrants may exert on the prestige of jobs held by natives, and for 1980, on native SES.

Analysis are limited to three panels, 1960, 1970, and 1980. The dependent variable is average American prestige, and for 1980, average American socioeconomic attainment. The independent variables include: percentage of immigrants, average educational attainment, percentage female, average age, and percentage non-white.

Findings on the impact of immigration on the occupational prestige and SES of native born Americans are given in Table 7.3. Immigrants made significant positive contributions to native occupational prestige in 1970. In both 1960 and 1980, they had no significant influence on native prestige or SES. The results seem to imply that immigrants do not hurt natives in terms of occupational prestige or socioeconomic status.

At the micro level, it was found that immigrants tended to go into less prestigious occupations in the 1960 to 1970 period, and they went into higher status jobs in the 1970 and 1980 period. These patterns do not seem to have hurt natives in any discernible way. The most consistent finding across all three panels is the impact of education on occupational prestige and SES. In 1960, a year's increase in average number of schooling completed led to a 3.7 increase in average prestige scores. Comparable figures were 3.15 in 1970, and for SES, 4.82 in 1980. Findings at the micro level for non-whites were repeated at the macro level. Non-whites exerted a negative influence on occupational prestige, suggesting that not only do minorities tend to be in low SES jobs, but their pattern of being in such occupations brings down the average socioeconomic attainment of the native population as a whole. Average educational levels were the strongest determinants of average American occupational prestige and SES. The significant variables were able to explain 61 percent and 54 percent respectively of the variance in native occupational prestige in 1960 and 1970, and 71 percent of the variance in SES in 1980.

As before, separate analysis was done on states having disproportionately large numbers of immigrants to see if results obtained for the country as a whole would hold true in those states. Five percent was used as the cutoff point for additional analysis. Results of the analysis are presented in Appendix D.

Findings on the effects of immigration are not much different from those reported for the whole country in Table 7.3. Taking other factors into account, immigrants made positive contributions to the occupational prestige of natives in the 1960 to 1970 decade (as reflected in the 1970 data). They had no significant effects in the 1960 panel. As in earlier findings, educational attainment levels had the single most important impact on occupational prestige and SES, and the results hold true for all time panels.

Metropolitan Results of the Effects of immigration on native socioeconomic attainment, 1980

Results on the impact of immigration on native SES in Metropolitan Statistical Areas are presented in Table 7.4. Findings are based on the 1 percent (1980) B sample. Other variables controlled include average weeks worked, percent non-white, percent females, and average educational attainment. The unstandardized regression coefficient of the

Table 7.3 Impact of Immigration on Native Prestige (1960 - 1970), and on Native Socioeconomic Attainment (1980)

Independent Variable	Native Job Prestige			Native SES
	1960	1970		1980
Pct. Immigrants				
Std. estimate	.061[@]	.224[a]		.116[c]
t-ratio	.087	.340		.143
	.871	3.173		1.516
Pct. Female				
Std. estimate	.298[a]	.166		.219[b]
t-ratio	.348	.103		.197
	3.635	.915		2.232
Average Weeks Worked				
Std. estimate	.178	.597[a]		.048
t-ratio	.109	.386		.035
	1.151	3.770		.428
Pct. Non-white				
Std. estimate	.019	.051		-.045[a]
t-ratio	.059	.141		-.159
	.544	1.325		-1.748
Average Education				
Std. estimate	3.929[a]	3.151[a]		4.823[a]
t-ratio	.686	.536		.830
	6.139	5.056		9.340
R^2	.613	.540		.711
Adj. R^2	.570	.488		.679
Number of Observations	51	51		51

a significant at $p < .01$. (one-tailed test).
b significant at $p < .05$. (one-tailed test).
c significant at $p < .10$. (one-tailed test)
@ unstandardized estimate

effects of immigration on native SES was .104, the standardized estimate was .219, and the *t*-statistic was 7.010. The unstandardized estimate shows that a one percent increase in immigration in a metropolitan area led to an increase of .10 points on average in the socioeconomic attainment of native born Americans. If the beta weights are rank-ordered in terms of size, immigration would be the third most important determinant of native SES.

The effects of the other variables in the equation in Table 7.4 are worth mentioning. As might be expected, education was the single most important predictor of native SES. A one year increase in MSA educational level on average raised native SES scores by 3.436 points. Percent non-white appears unrelated to native SES. Percent females in MSA had moderate effects on native socioeconomic attainment. Average number of weeks worked in an MSA led to higher SES.

The foregoing may in part be a reflection of the prevalence of full-time as opposed to part-time workers in an MSA. Full-time workers are more likely to work more weeks during the year than part-time workers. Furthermore, full-time workers are more likely to be in jobs with higher SES than part-time workers. Thus, to the extent that an MSA has more persons working full-time than part-time, it is likely to benefit in terms of higher than average increases in SES. The significant variables in the equation in Table 7.4 together explained nearly 94 percent of the variance in native socioeconomic attainment.

The above findings suggest that in terms of native SES, immigration appears to have beneficial effects on the United States. If in fact there are beneficial consequences, then they should be evident in metropolitan areas with above average immigrant populations.

Appendix E presents regression results based on MSAs with immigrants 10% or more of the population. The sample size is 25 cases. The unstandardized regression coefficient for the effects of immigrants is .081, the standardized coefficient is .178, and the t-statistic is 3.455. A comparison of these figures and those on Table 7.4 indicate that there is some attenuation in the positive effects of immigration on native SES in metropolitan areas having higher than average numbers of immigrants. At the same time, however, immigration continues to lead to increases in native socioeconomic status. Percent females in MSA is now unrelated to native SES. Percent non-white is marginally, but negatively related to native SES. The latter finding could mean that in metropolitan areas having above average immigrant populations, immigrants may be taking over jobs previously filled by minorities.

Table 7.4   Metropolitan Level Analysis of the Effects of Immigration on Native Socioeconomic Status, 1980

Independent Variables	b	Beta	t-value	Prob.
Percent Immigrants	.104	.219	7.010	.000
Average Weeks Worked	.650	.401	10.832	.000
Percent Non-white	.004	.013	.424	.336
Percent Females	.138	.058	1.775	.040
Average Educational Attainment	3.436	.626	17.454	.000
R^2		.939		
Adj. R^2		.935		
Number of Observations		76		

As such jobs are taken away, native minorities fall into even lower status occupations. The results imply that minorities may not benefit from increases in immigration. Rather, the main beneficiaries of immigration into the United States may be the white majority.

As before, average number of weeks worked in 1979 was a significant predictor of native SES in 1980. Education remained the most important determinant of native socioeconomic attainment. The significant variables explained 94 percent of the variance in the dependent variable.

Chapter 8

The Effects of Immigration
on Industrial Sector

A fundamental assumption in much of the past literature dealing with the effects of immigration on the U.S. labor market is that immigrants are in the secondary labor market wherein they compete with natives, especially minorities. Indeed, the competitive, substitutive relation between immigrants and minorities, is a fundamental assumption of dual labor market theory. To determine whether immigrants displace natives in the secondary labor market, it is essential to first provide empirical evidence indicating whether or not immigrants are in that market.

The dependent variable in this chapter is industrial sector. As discussed elsewhere, it is based on industrial segmentation scores derived from Tolbert, Horan, and Beck (1980). Past researchers studying the dual economy theory have classified industries into core and periphery economic sectors rather arbitrarily. Bibb and Form, for example (1977) assigned industries to core and periphery based on narrative descriptions found in past literature. Beck, Horan, and Tolbert (1978) classified industries into core and periphery in a similar manner. In short, past studies have divided the economy into two sectors and argued that the characteristics of these sectors imply different labor market outcomes for persons in the different sectors.

Kaufman and Hodson (1981) have identified the need to extend this 'dualistic' approach and take other aspects of the economy into account. They propose a perspective whereby industries are not just classified according to outcomes of individuals in them, but based on the general resources of the industries concerned. Kaufman and Hodson (1981:16) divide the economy into oligopoly sector, core sector, wholesale sector, periphery small shop sector, core utilities and finance sector, and periphery utilities sector; core transport sector, periphery transport sector, local monopoly sector, education and nonprofit sector, agricultural sector, brokers, real estate, and tobacco sector.

In an attempt to measure economic segmentation, Tolbert, Horan, and Beck (1980:1099) grouped multiple indicators of industrial oligopoly into three general categories. These include: (1) measures of the capacity for oligopoly in an industry, (2) measures of oligopolistic behavior in the industrial product market, and (3) measures of oligopolistic behavior in the industrial labor market. Their first group of variables includes factors reflecting the potential for exercising oligopolistic market power, especially market concentration, economic scale, and barriers to entry. The core sector is viewed as one in which industries act upon their capacity through oligopolistic behavior in industrial product and labor markets. They used profit levels, industry levels of political contributions, and advertising expenditures as indicators of oligopolistic behavior.

Their measure is relevant for the present analysis because it assumes an underlying dimension which is common to all indicators, and which show patterns of relationships predicted by dual labor market theory. A further advantage is that unlike some past studies that create a dummy variable to indicate core (1) and periphery (0) segmentation scores used are interval level data. High scores on industrial sector denote greater oligopolistic or "coreness" tendencies of the industry in which a given individual is employed. Low scores indicate peripheral tendencies of the industry. Thus, a variable that is positively related to industrial sector is a reflection of covariation between it and tendency towards oligopoly and core. A negative relationship is interpreted as an indication of the periphery or secondary labor market. For issues of industrial data comparability, analysis is limited to 1960, 1970, and 1980.

Effects of Immigrant Status on Industrial Sector, 1960 to 1980

Findings in Table 8.1 show that immigrant status has negative effects on industrial sector, and these results hold true for all three time panels. The unstandardized coefficients are -5.08, -11.32, and -1.83 in

Table 8.1.

Determinants of Industrial Sector, 1960 - 1980

Independent Variable	1960			1970			1980		
	b	Beta	t	b	Beta	t	b	Beta	t
Weeks Worked	2.00	.28	77.1	1.14	.11	29.5	2.82	.40	154.0
Immigrant Status	-5.08	-.06	-19.6	-11.32	-.16	-46.8	-1.83	-.02	-8.3
Race	-5.08	-.06	-19.3	-4.40	-.07	-18.8	1.46	.02	9.0
Age	-.16	-.08	-3.7	.18	.12	4.4	.57	.32	17.8
Region	.59	.01	3.6	.54	.01	3.6	-1.14	-.02	-9.6
Children	-.38	-.02	-7.2	-.08	-.01	-1.6	.00	.00	0.1
Marital	-2.80	-.04	-14.0	-5.16	-.11	-29.0	-1.67	-.03	-12.4
Education	.09	.01	3.4	.49	.07	19.2	.48	.06	22.6
Sex	-6.08	-.12	-32.6	-6.59	-.15	-42.3	-7.90	-.17	-65.3
Age Square	-.00	-.02	-1.0	-.00	-.13	-4.9	-.00	-.34	-18.5
R²		.14			.11			.26	
N		95,803			75,305			130,868	

1960, 1970, and 1980 respectively. Corresponding beta weights are -.06 (1960), -.16 (1970), and -.02 (1980). These negative findings imply that during the years studied, immigrants were significantly more likely than natives to be in the secondary labor market.

Results of the effects of other variables are reported. Non-whites appear to be in the secondary labor market in 1960 and 1970, but they do not appear to be there in 1980. States (regions) with heavy immigrant concentrations tended to have core and oligopolistic industries in 1960 and 1970. Results were, however, different in 1980. The negative signs observed during 1980 seem to imply fewer core industries in those states, and more peripheral industries. Older individuals tended to be in core industries in 1970 and 1980, but not in 1960. Single, divorced, separated and widowed individuals appear to be over represented in the secondary labor market in all time panels, but especially so in 1970. In general, educated individuals were in core or oligopolistic industries. The negative coefficients on sex in Table 8.1 show that women are consistently in the secondary labor market. All coefficients on sex seem to gain strength over the years. In 1960, the beta weight was -.12; in 1970 it was -.15, and in 1980, it stood at -.17. The significant variables in the equation in Table 8.1 were able to explain 14 percent of the variance in industrial sector in 1960, 11 percent in 1970, and 26 percent in 1980.

As in past models, potentially relevant variables were not controlled in the model in Table 8.1. It is thus possible that perhaps some of the results obtained in Table 8.1 could be due to the omission of such variables. In Table 8.2, other variables were taken into account, and analysis was done on the 1 percent (B) sample of the 1980 Census. Additional variables added to the equation include work disability, alien status, years since immigration, and English proficiency. Table 8.2 presents findings based on the expanded model.

Results of the expanded model are no different from those obtained earlier in 1980. The percent of variance explained by the equation remained the same at about 26%. Immigrants are still more likely than whites to be in the secondary labor market. In addition, aliens (non citizens) also appear to be in the secondary labor market. Years since immigration has no effect on industrial sector. Those with work disability are likely to be in secondary labor markets. As in the Demographics of Aging File sample for 1980, results in Table 8.2 show race positively related to industrial sector, suggesting that non-whites are significantly more likely than whites to be in secondary labor markets.

Table 8.2

Determinants of Industrial Sector, 1980

Independent Variable	b	Beta	t-ratio	Prob.
Weeks Worked	.429	.407	244.56	.000
Immigrant Status	-1.144	-.016	-4.73	.000
Alien Status	-.482	-.005	-2.23	.025
Race	.843	.015	9.56	.000
Age	.753	.450	42.20	.000
Square of Age	-.009	-.437	-41.50	.000
Region	-.351	-.007	-4.91	.000
Children under 18	-.170	-.010	-6.41	.000
Marital Status	-1.858	-.039	-21.82	.000
Education	.546	.076	47.10	.000
Sex	-5.961	-.127	-83.05	.000
Work Disability	-1.563	-.019	-12.25	.000
Years Since Immigration	.005	.001	.47	.639
English Proficiency	-.197	-.006	-3.02	.003
R^2		.265		
Number of Observations		347,665		

Such an interpretation, however, would be a refutation of an important assumption of dual labor market theory, the view that minority workers tend to be over represented in the secondary sector. A more probably explanation is that in the 1970 to 1980 decade, non-whites made some advances into key core industries, such as automobiles, and their presence there influenced the 1980 data.

Effects of immigration on Native Industrial Sector, 1960 to 1980

It was shown in the previous section that immigrants were more likely than natives to be in secondary (periphery) labor markets, at least in 1960 and 1970. The next issue to address involves the consequences on the American (native born) population. To determine the effects of immigration on native industrial sector, aggregate analysis are performed in this section. The dependent variable is average industrial sector. The independent variables include percentage immigrants, percentage female, percentage non-white, average educational attainment, and average number of weeks worked. Initially, results are presented for the whole country, and then states with above average immigrant populations are studied separately. Five percent or more is the cutoff point. Due to data limitations, analysis are limited to 1960, 1970, and 1980.

Table 8.3 presents macro level results on the impact of immigration on native industrial sector. As seen from these findings, in 1970 a one-percent increase in immigration was associated with an average increase of .332% in native industrial sector. In 1980, the comparable figure was .321. The evidence suggests that some sort of 'industrial succession' is at work, whereby immigrants take jobs in the secondary labor market and then natives take jobs located in core or oligopolistic sectors of the economy. The findings seem to add credence to past observations in the literature that in the United States, there is a tendency for immigrants to take jobs that natives do not want. These jobs tend to be found mainly in the peripheral sector of the economy, in secondary labor markets. These remarks are not to be viewed as an approval of such jobs. Some may argue that perhaps these jobs should not exist in the first place. Still others might charge that by going into secondary labor market jobs, immigrants tend to compete with minorities that are also located there. However, this line of thinking is itself flawed. It assumes that secondary labor market jobs are exclusively for minorities, who are often expected to perform jobs that nobody else wants. Perhaps a better way to interpret

Table 8.3   Effects of immigration on Native Industrial Scent, 1960 - 1980

Independent Variable	1960	1970	1980
Percentage Immigrants			
Std. estimate	.246[c]	.332[a]	.321[a]
	.232	.482	.430
t-ratio	1.553	3.980	2.853
Percentage Female			
Std. estimate	-.146	.283	-.107
	-.112	.168	-.106
t-ratio	-.776	1.317	-.746
Percentage Non-white			
Std. estimate	-.018	-.013	-.038
	-.036	-.034	-.149
t-ratio	-.221	-.290	-1.021
Average Education			
Std. estimate	-.069	1.856[a]	.631
	-.008	.301	.120
t-ratio	-.048	2.517	.844
Average Weeks Worked			
Std. estimate	.534[c]	.542[a]	.300[b]
	.218	.334	.238
t-ratio	1.528	2.891	1.822
R^2 .125	.414	.258	.176
Adj. R^2	.026	.349	
Number of Observations	51	51	51

a significant at $p < .01$. (one-tailed test).
b significant at $p < .05$. (one-tailed test).
c significant at $p < .10$. (one-tailed test).

these results is that some sort of occupational mobility takes place among the native born, with immigrants 'pushing them up in the industrial hierarchy.

Prior analysis above showed that immigrants make significant positive contributions to the sector of natives in industry. To further investigate this issue, separate analysis was performed on states with above average number of immigrants. Findings of this analysis are presented in Appendix F. Results show that even in states with considerable numbers of immigrants, the latter do not appear to have adverse effects on natives. In 1960 and 1980, immigration had no significant effects on native industrial sector. However, in the 1970 panel, a standard deviation increase in immigration led to a 49 percent standard deviation change in native industrial sector, holding constant the effects of other variables in the equation. In terms of standard deviation unit changes in the dependent variable, immigration was the most important determinant of native industrial sector in the 1970 panel.

The above results, combined with those presented in Table 8.3 confirm that perhaps immigrants push up natives in the industrial ladder, from the periphery to core or more oligopolistic sectors. It may be, as suggested earlier, that immigrants take up low-paying dead-end jobs that natives either vacate or do not like. These findings support Piore's (1979) contention that in industrial societies, certain jobs are unwanted by natives. These are often located in secondary (peripheral) sectors of the economy. Immigrants tend to accept them until such a time as they are able to move socially into more higher paying and stable jobs.

Although statistically insignificant, the negative results for the 1980 panel suggest that above average concentrations of immigrants could have some negative effects on natives in terms of industrial sectors of employment.

Effects of Immigration on Change in Native Industrial Sector, 1970 to 1980

The foregoing results showed that immigrants tend to be over represented in the secondary labor market. Apart from studying the likelihood of competition that might arise between them and minorities, it may be useful to determine the extent to which changes in immigration over a given decade might influence changes in native industrial sector. To perform such an investigation, change in the percentage of immigrants was related to change in native industrial sector for the period 1970 to 1980.

Results of the analysis of the impact of change in immigration on change in native industrial sector are presented in Table 8.4. Findings show that a one percent increase in immigration between 1970 and 1980 moved natives up the industrial ladder by .290 points, controlling for the effects of other variables in the equation. The evidence seems to suggest that native born Americans as a whole did not suffer as a consequence of immigration during the 1970-1980 decade. It should be pointed out, however, that whatever dividends of immigration that might have existed in 1970 to 1980 did not benefit all groups in America. Minorities, for example are in competition with some immigrant groups. It is therefore, improbable that non-whites would have derived much benefit from immigration during the period under study. The extent to which immigration might have hurt minority groups in the United States is investigated in the next chapter.

Metropolitan Results of the Effects of Immigration on Native Industrial sector, 1980

In the analysis of the impact of immigration in states with substantially higher percentages of immigrants, it was found that the latter might have some negative effects. A focus on metropolitan areas might help to further investigate this possibility. Table 8.5 presents findings on the effects of immigration on native industrial sector. The analysis was based on 76 MSAs.

Percentage immigrants appears unrelated to native industrial sector, but the coefficient is in the negative direction. Of the other variables in the equation, percentage non-white has marginal and negative effects on native industrial sector. Average number of weeks worked has the strongest impact on native industrial sector. The significant variables in the equation together explained almost 54 percent of the variance in the dependent variable.

The equation in Table 8.5 was estimated on MSAs with immigrants 10% or more of the population. Results of this analysis are shown in Appendix G. Immigration had no impact on native industrial sector, and the coefficient continued to be in the negative direction. An increase of one percent of females in MSAs with 10 percent or more immigrants reduced native industrial sector by .88 points on average. Average number of weeks worked is the most important predictor of industrial sector. An increase in the number of weeks worked increases native industrial sector by 1.373 points. Percentage non-white, average educational attainment, and percentage with work disability were unrelated to native industrial sector.

Table 8.4   Effects of Immigration on Change in Native Industrial Sector, 1970 - 1980

Independent Variable	b	Beta	t-ratio	Prob.
Change in Immigration	.290	.153[b]	1.897	.0322
Change in Weeks Worked	.318	.264[b]	1.725	.0458
Change in Divorce	-.004	-.008	-0.054	.4786
Change in College Education	.078	.233[c]	1.475	.0736
Change in Pct. Female	.128	.146	0.772	.2222
Change in Average Age	-.106	-.048	-0.229	.4100
R^2		.183		
Adj. R^2		.072		
Number of Observations		51		

a Significant at $p < .01$ (one-tailed test).
b Significant at $p < .05$ (one-tailed test).
c Significant at $p < .10$ (one-tailed test).

Table 8.5   Metropolitan Level Analysis of the Effects of Immigration on Native Industrial Sector, 1980

Independent Variable	b	Beta	t-value	Prob.
Percent Immigrants	-.019	-.047	-.526	.300
Average Weeks Worked	.798	.579	4.196	.000
Percent Non-white	-.301	-.130	-1.535	.064
Percent Females	-.219	-.109	-1.232	.111
Average Educational Attainment	-.679	-.145	-1.322	.095
Percent with Work Disability	-.296	-.238	-1.423	.080
R^2		.573		
Adj. R^2		.536		
Number of Observations			76	

Chapter 9

Effects of Immigration on Unemployment

The belief that immigrants displace natives by taking away jobs from them is strongly held by some U.S. policy makers and the general public. Unfortunately, much of the past research on whether or not immigrants displace natives remains inconclusive. In this chapter, an attempt is made to address the issue of whether increases in immigration reduce employment opportunities for natives. To test for displacement, unemployment is used as the dependent variable. If immigrants displace natives, then there should be increases in unemployment among natives as immigration increases. Furthermore, the displacing effects of immigration should be most pronounced in states or Metropolitan with above average concentrations of immigrants.

The first section of this chapter investigates general determinants of unemployment at the individual level. In the second section, aggregate results of the effects of immigration on unemployment levels of Americans in general, and native minorities are presented. I also look at the effects of growth in immigration between 1970 and 1980 on increases in unemployment during the same period. The assumption guiding the analysis in the second section is that if immigrants displace natives, then the effects of such displacement would be felt most by minorities. The rationale for this is based on past research findings, and on analysis in the previous chapter that indicated that both immigrants and minorities tend to be disproportionately represented in secondary labor markets.

Effects of Immigrant Status on Unemployment, 1940 to 1980

Results of analysis for the effects of immigrant status on unemployment are presented in Table 9.1. Note that at the individual level, unemployment is treated as a dummy variable whereby persons not in the labor force were given a code of 1, and those in the labor force were given a code of 0. The data reveal that immigrants were more likely to be unemployed than natives. This result holds true across various the time panels, except in 1950, when immigrant status appeared unrelated to unemployment.

Results for other variables reveal that non-whites were more likely than whites to be unemployed in 1970 and 1980. Non-whites were less likely to be unemployed than whites in 1940, 1950, and 1960. The pattern changed in 1970 and 1980. Besides competition from immigrants, there may well have been other external factors responsible for this dramatic reversal after 1960. Among others, the economic boom and prosperity of earlier decades gave way to an economic bust and recessions in the 1970's. Economic difficulties and government policies might thus in part be responsible for unemployment among minorities in 1970 and 1980, and not just immigration.

The most consistent findings in Table 9.1 are in connection with sex and education. Women were more likely to be unemployed and out of the labor force for all time panels considered, but with coefficients weakening over the decades, indicating greater tendency among females to enter the labor force in the 1960s and 1970s. Persons with higher educational levels were more likely to be employed than unemployed from 1940 through 1980, a hardly surprising finding.

Immigrant Status and Unemployment, 1980

As in past models, potentially relevant variables were not controlled in the model above. Perhaps some of the results obtained in Table 9.1 may be due to the omission of such variables. In Table 9.2, other variables were taken into account, and analysis was done on the 1 percent (B) sample of the 1980 Census. Additional variables added to the equation include work disability, public transportation disability, years since immigration, and English proficiency. Table 9.2 presents findings of the expanded model. Results are based on logistic regression. For comparative purposes, OLS estimates are shown in Appendix H.

Table 9.1

Determinants of Unemployment, 1940 - 1980

Independent Variable	1940	1950	1960	1970	1980
Immigrant Status	.050	-.006	.044	.022	.010
Std. estimate	.011	-.003	.027	.020	.006
t-ratio	4.677	-1.125	9.509	5.594	2.076
Race	-.092	-.046	-.039	.014	.059
Std. estimate	-.053	-.062	-.025	.013	.046
t-ratio	-17.524	-9.454	-8.648	3.675	16.969
Age	.000	-.000	-.002	-.003	.002
Std. estimate	.003	-.009	-.042	-.102	.057
t-ratio	1.060	-2.930	-13.498	-26.427	19.910
Region	-.022	-.013	-.021	-.008	.004
Std. estimate	-.021	-.012	-.020	-.011	.004
t-ratio	-7.046	-4.272	-7.302	-3.103	1.512
Children	.012	.013	.010	.002	.009
Std. estimate	.038	.040	.034	.009	.024
t-ratio	12.282	13.431	11.161	2.319	8.788
Marital	-.072	-.069	-.040	.023	-.002
Std. estimate	-.067	-.062	-.035	.032	-.002
t-ratio	-21.798	-21.261	-11.925	8.342	-.788
Education	-.010	-.008	-.015	-.006	-.029
Std. estimate	-.067	-.057	-.102	-.057	-.184
t-ratio	-21.118	-18.788	-34.070	-15.179	-68.173
Sex	.551	.531	.483	.116	.253
Std. estimate	.554	.537	.497	.172	.275
t-ratio	188.904	191.108	178.540	47.405	106.145
R^2	.321	.298	.259	.047	.126
N	79.237	89.019	95.803	75.305	130.868

Ideally, logistic techniques are more desirable when the dependent variable is categorical. However, its prohibitive cost in the face of a large number of observations and several independent variables makes its use a pragmatic deterrence in the foregoing analysis. Furthermore, logistic results are often similar to OLS ones. There are 347,665 observations in the 1980 sample. A 5% probability subsample was selected from this, and the resulting 17,424 cases were used. The dependent variable is represented by the expression $P(Y=1)$. The estimated value of the variable may be interpreted as the probability (or odds) that an individual respondent was unemployed in 1980. Each logit coefficient is a measure of the amount of effect expected on the log of the odds of the dependent variable for a unit change in an independent variable (Kposowa, 1995).

The column labeled **b** in Table 9.2 is the logit coefficient or the log of the odds of being unemployed. Results show that immigrant status is only marginally related to the odds of unemployment. The logit coefficient (.190) indicates that being an immigrant increased the odds of being unemployed by .190. Alien status appears unrelated to the odds of unemployment.

Work disability and sex emerge as the most important predictors of unemployment. Work disability increases the odds of unemployment by 1.426, and sex increases the odds by 1.154. Semi-standardized coefficients in the third column measure the change in the log odds of the dependent variable for a standard deviation change in an independent variable (Kposowa, 1987b: 6, 1995). As a statistic, the semi-standardized estimate can be used for rank ordering the size of the various exogenous variables, without necessarily telling us the strength of individual coefficients. By rank ordering the variables in column 3, it is evident that sex is the most important, followed by work disability, education, and public transportation disability.

Effect of Immigration on Native Unemployment, 1940 to 1980

As was discussed at the beginning of this chapter, micro level analysis are incapable of probing the question of whether or not immigrants displace native workers. At best, results in the foregoing section are only useful to the extent that they reveal differences in unemployment patterns with regard to individuals. Their usefulness is therefore, limited from a policy point of view. Policy makers interested in immigration are often interested in knowing whether American citizens, especially the native born are displaced by the newcomers. Adequate investigation of this issue can be done only at the aggregate level.

This section presents findings on the impact of immigration on unemployment, with the latter being used as an indicator of

Table 9.2				Logistic Regression (ML) Results of the Probability of Unemployment, 1980	
Independent Variable	b	b(1-P)P	Semi Std. coeff.	Semi Std. Δ in P(Y=1)	t-ratio
Immigrant Status	.190	.042	.062	.014	1.568
Alien Status	-.020	-.004	-.005	-.001	-0.183
Education	-.126	-.028	-.407	-.083	-20.540
Marital Status	.177	.039	.087	.019	4.400
Race	-.004	-.001	-.002	-.001	-0.079
English Proficiency	.077	.017	.057	.013	2.298
Work Disability	1.426	.314	.413	.096	21.880
Pub. Transp. Disab.	1.003	.221	.138	.031	6.421
Years Since Immigr.	-.016	-.004	-.085	-.018	-2.942
Region	.056	.012	.027	.006	1.531
Age	-.002	-.001	-.028	-.006	-1.078
Children under 18	.264	.058	.132	.030	6.812
Sex	1.154	.254	.576	.137	31.590
Constant	-.205				

Log Likelihood = -9749.48.
Degrees of freedom = 13.
Pseudo R² = .127

Likelihood Ratio Statistic = 2540.87.
Sample mean of Y = .328.
Number of observations = 17,424

displacement. Results will be shown for the years 1940 to 1980 at the state level. Then additional analysis will be given at the MSA level for 1980. MSAs seem to be the ideal unit of analysis for this type of study. However, the *Demographics of Aging File* being used lacks MSA level data for all the years. Useful information can be aggregated at the MSA level for only 1980.

Findings in Table 9.3 seem to go against the argument that immigrants displace native workers. At the state level, in all the years under study, immigration had negative effects on unemployment of native born citizens in the United States. In 1940, for example, a percentage increase in immigration led to a .49% decline in American unemployment. Comparable figures were, -.577%, -.410%, -.535%, and -.523% in 1950, 1960, 1970, and 1980 respectively. It thus seems that when the country as a whole is considered, and when the native population is not disaggregated, immigration reduces, or seems to reduce unemployment. It is possible that these results are in part due to the fact that at the state level, levels of immigration are not very well pronounced. In 1980, for example, the average percentage of immigrants in the country was 5.9. It may be that different results would be obtained if states with large immigrant populations are considered. To investigate this possibility, different immigrant cutoff points were considered. The analysis was repeated for states with immigrant populations 5 percent or more.

Results of the analysis of the impact of immigration on native unemployment in states with immigrant populations of 5 percent or more are shown in Table 9.4. Note that for 1940, due to the small percentage of immigrants, (only 3.2), a different cutoff point was used. When 5 percent was used the sample was reduced to only 10 states. Since it would be meaningless to do any useful multivariate analysis on only 10 cases, 1 percent was used as cutoff. This increased the sample to 19 cases.

Results in Table 9.4 are not much different from those reported earlier. Immigration still has negative effects on native unemployment, with decreased magnitude in coefficients. The question arises as to what the findings mean. On the one hand, these results constitute evidence that immigrants do not displace the native born. On the other hand, it could be that immigrants do displace some groups, but these displacing effects are masked when all groups are considered together. Immigrants may not be substitutes for the entire population, but they may be substitutes and competitors for sub groups within the population. The next section investigates the impact of immigration on minority unemployment.

Table 9.3

Effects of Immigration on Unemployment Among Native Born Americans

Independent Variable	1940	1950	1960	1970	1980
Pct. Immigrants@	-.493	-.577a	-.410a	-.535a	-.523a
Std. estimate	-.310	-.311	-.344	-.438	-.370
t-ratio	-2.457	-3.046	-2.457	-3.944	-2.401
Average Age	-.427	-.879c	.246	-2.055a	-.667
Std. estimate	-.125	-.155	.046	-.391	-.121
t-ratio	-1.105	-1.583	.265	-3.034	-.824
Pct. Female	-.427a	1.040a	-.632a	1.075a	-.056
Std. estimate	-.450	.786	-.434	.357	-.029
t-ratio	-3.703	8.853	-3.129	2.531	-.197
Pct. Non-white	-.234b	-.276a	.084	-.241a	-.006
Std. estimate	-.267	-.288	.151	-.361	-.013
t-ratio	-1.965	-2.939	.952	-3.197	-.087
Pct. with Less Than High School Educat.	-.032	.201b	.030	.171c	.464b
Std. estimate	-.040	.203	.040	.159	.327
t-ratio	-.310	2.049	.262	1.455	2.312
R^2	.498	.688	.330	.515	.276
Adj. R^2	.440	.652	.255	.461	.195
Number of Observations	49	49	51	51	51

a coefficient significant at $p < .01$ (one-tailed test).
b coefficient significant at $p < .05$ (one-tailed test).
c coefficient significant at $p < .10$ (one-tailed test).
@ unstandardized estimate

Table 9.4   Effects of Immigration on Native Unemployment, States with Immigrant populations 5% or more

Independent Variable	1940	1950	1960	1970	1980
Pct. immigrants	-.709[b]	-.561[a]	-.452[b]	-.795[a]	-.739[b]
Std. estimate	-.619	-.389	-.408	-.552	-.478
t-ratio	-1.986	-2.333	-2.064	-4.698	-1.883
Pct. females	.116	.378	.351	.569	.851
Std. estimate	.156	.228	.260	.143	.401
t-ratio	.521	1.383	.874	1.179	1.255
Average age	.034	-2.997[a]	-1.197	-2.163[a]	1.071
Std. estimate	.010	-.511	-.292	-.381	.184
t-ratio	.041	-3.044	-.987	-3.066	.629
Pct. non-white	-.147	-.319[a]	-.124	-.295[a]	-.092
Std. estimate	-.132	-.401	-.335	-.500	-.246
t-ratio	-.537	-2.369	-1.007	-4.056	-1.059
Pct. with less than high school educat					
Std. estimate	-.001	.074	.004	.234[b]	-.042
	-.002	.097	.005	.207	-.028
t-ratio	-.008	.587	.023	1.778	-.122
R^2	.472	.545	.190	.702	.263
Adj. R^2	.268	.419	.006	.638	.069
Number of Observations	19	24	28	29	25

a significant at p < .01.
b significant at p < .05.
c significant at p < .10.

The Effect of Immigration on U.S. Minorities, 1940 to 1980

If immigrants displace natives, then this displacement might be felt most among minorities. Furthermore, if skill levels of immigrants have declined as some analysts have found, then the displacing effects of immigration on native minorities should be most evident in 1980s, and to a lesser extent in the 1970s. Minorities are classified as non-white groups as a whole. To determine whether the foregoing propositions are true, the possible impact of immigration on minority unemployment was investigated, using percentage of native non-whites unemployed as the dependent variable. Results of the analysis using this disaggregated group are shown in Table 9.5.

Immigration was positively related to minority unemployment rates in 1950, 1960, 1970, and 1980. However, immigration had no statistically significant effects on minority unemployment except in 1970 and 1980.   In 1970, a one percent increase in the percentage of immigrants in a state led to .066 percentage increase in the percentage of non-whites out of work.   These results appear to suggest that immigrants displaced some minorities, at least in the 1960 to 1970 decade.   These results however warrant further examination. Since immigrants appear to displace native non-whites, perhaps the observed displacement patterns will be more consistent and severe if we focus on states with a higher percentage of immigrants.

Before pursuing this, however, it may be of interest to dwell briefly on some of the other findings in Table 9.5. Results show that in 1960 and 1980, females appear to have displaced minorities in employment. Putting the findings in some historical context might explain the female effect.   The 1960 to 1970 decade experienced increasing female labor force participation.   The same holds for the 1970 to 1980 decade. Perhaps as more females entered the labor force,
the casualties of that trend in the work force were minority groups that lost jobs. The findings imply that not only are immigrants and minorities substitutes and competitors in the labor market, but females and minorities are also substitutes and competitors.

A consistent and disturbing finding in Table 9.5 is the persistent effect of low minority skill level on unemployment among minority groups. Minority skill level was measured as the percentage of native non-whites that had no education, or that had not completed high school. Results show that one of the main causes of unemployment among minorities may be an inability of these groups to improve on their human

Table 9.5   Effects of Immigration on Unemployment Among American Minorities, 1940 - 1980

Independent Variable	1940	1950	1960	1970	1980
Pct. Immigrants					
Std. estimate	-.039@	.029	.038	.066[a]	.085[c]
t-ratio	-.058	.039	.051	.140	.097
	-1.325	.934	.868	2.346	1.472
Pct. Female					
Std. estimate	.003	.018	.098[b]	.090	.131[b]
t-ratio	.008	.034	.109	.078	.110
	.205	.825	2.016	1.123	1.706
Percent Minorities With no Skill					
Std. estimate	.401[a]	.496[a]	.630[a]	.818[a]	1.591[a]
t-ratio	.953	.950	.859	.886	.823
	25.616	23.201	13.771	12.464	12.767
Pct. Divorced					
Std. estimate	.020	.118[a]	.102[a]	.042	.135[a]
t-ratio	.019	.105	.174	.053	.180
	.485	2.608	3.005	.814	2.705
Pct. less than 25					
Std. estimate	.016	-.004	.071[b]	-.002	.044
t-ratio	.037	-.007	.094	-.004	.069
	1.007	-.175	1.708	-.061	1.031
R²	.946	.939	.871	.854	.826
Adj. R²	.940	.932	.857	.838	.807
Number of Observations	49	49	51	51	51

a significant at p < .01. (one-tailed test).
b significant at p < .05. (one-tailed test).
c significant at p < .10. (one-tailed test).
@ unstandardized estimate

capital. This should not be construed as an effort to blame the victim. Many minority groups in the United States, especially African Americans have been subjected to all forms of discrimination and prejudice that have translated into inferior education or no education at all, and general reduction in human capital. These factors in turn have translated into unemployment and low labor force participation. However, the present data do not permit us to investigate the effects of discrimination.

To further investigate whether immigrants displace natives by affecting their unemployment levels, states with 5 percent or more of immigrants were analyzed separately. Results of the analysis are outlined in Table 9.6. Findings show that immigrants displace native minorities. The coefficients are all in the positive direction, except for 1940 and 1960. The displacing effects were strongest in the 1940 to 1950 decade which are reflected in the 1950 results. During that decade, findings show that for every one percent increase in immigration, there was a corresponding increase of .113 in percentage of native non-whites unemployed.

These results indicate that the displacing effects of immigration are small nationally, but in states with large immigrant populations and groups, the potential for serious displacement, leading to considerable harm to various minority groups exists. Accordingly, the possible consequences in terms of the national interest should not be underestimated.

Minority unemployment is persistently a function of low skill levels in that group. The implications of this are very serious. For a start, it seems that some of the displacing effects of immigration would be reduced if members of minority groups would improve on their human capital. The results show that the groups most affected by immigrants are those with lower levels of education, and therefore, those with the least ability to compete. Findings in Table 9.6 further suggest that whether or not immigrants displace minorities depends on the general economic health of the United States. In periods of economic boom, displacement is either small or absent. But in times of economic bust, displacement appears more serious. The 1940 to 1950 period represent a time of great economic hardships in the United States, following the end of the Second World War in 1945. This is reflected in the strong positive effects of immigration on minority unemployment during that decade. The 1950 to 1960 decade was, however, a time of economic recovery, and so immigration had no effect on native minority unemployment. In fact, the coefficients for immigration were in the

Table 9.6   Effects of Immigration on Native Minority Unemployment, States with 5% or More Immigrants, 1940 - 1980

Independent Variable	1940	1950	1960	1970	1980
Pct. Immigrants					
Std. estimate	-.022	.113[a]	-.062	.042	.111
t-ratio	-.059	.203	-.083	.098	.097
	-.948	3.016	-.902	.871	1.037
Pct. Females					
Std. estimate	.008	.000	.233[b]	-.052	.278[b]
t-ratio	.035	.000	.256	-.044	.176
	.366	.0092	.094	-.376	1.830
Percent Minorities With no Skill					
Std. estimate	.394[a]	.463[a]	.885[a]	.865[a]	1.503[a]
t-ratio	.957	.798	.649	.795	.736
	22.006	9.836	4.831	5.326	7.036
Pct. Divorced					
Std. estimate	-.008	.164[a]	.098	.070	.209[b]
t-ratio	-.015	.228	.142	.113	.213
	-.329	2.775	1.399	.817	1.860
Pct. less than 25					
Std. estimate	.014	-.039	.110[c]	.028	.064
t-ratio	.044	-.088	.165	.069	.080
	.587	-1.364	1.540	.615	.833
R^2	.979	.927	.826	.740	.874
Adj. R^2	.971	.906	.787	.683	.841
Number of Observations	19	24	28	29	25

a   significant at $p < .01$. (one-tailed test)
b   significant at $p < .05$. (one-tailed test)
c   significant at $p < .10$. (one-tailed test)

negative direction in 1960. Despite some difficulties, the economy experienced a boom in the 1960 to 1970 period, so immigration again had no effect on minority unemployment in that decade. In the 1970 to 1980 period, however, the United States experienced a severe economic recession, and so once again, immigration seems to have had a positive, that is, an increasing effect on minority unemployment.

Effects of Change in Immigration on Change in Native unemployment, 1970 to 1980

Earlier findings in this chapter showed that natives as a whole are not adversely affected by immigration. To further investigate the issue, change scores for the independent variables were computed and related to growth in native unemployment. Analysis is limited to the 1970 to 1980 period for reasons already indicated.

This section presents regression results of the impact of change in immigration from 1970 to 1980 on change in native unemployment for the same period. Findings in Table 9.7 reveal that a change in immigration from 1970 to 1980 had a negative impact on growth in native unemployment. A one percent increase in immigration during 1970 to 1980 led to a .52 percent reduction in native unemployment, and this result is statistically significant at the 95% level of confidence. The beta weight (-.28) indicates that a one standard deviation increment in immigration during the decade was associated with a .28 standard deviation decrease in native unemployment levels. These results again appear to confirm that for native born Americans as a whole, immigrants do not pose a threat in terms of job loss.

Effects of Change in Immigration on Change in Minority Unemployment, 1970 to 1980

While the foregoing findings show that immigration is not detrimental to all American jobs, there may be some segments of the native population who may lose jobs as a consequence of increases in immigration. Prior analysis have already found that immigrants displace minorities. Analysis of the impact of change in immigration on change in minority unemployment might further reveal the extent to which minorities lose jobs as a consequence of increases in immigration.

Results in Table 9.8 show that a 1% change in immigration between 1970 and 1980 led to a corresponding .13% increase in minority

Table 9.7   Effects of Change in Immigration on Change in Native Unemployment, 1970 - 1980

Independent Variable	b	Beta	t-ratio	Prob.
Change in Immigration	-.517	-.281[b]	-1.804	.0389
Change in Pct. with less than High School Education	-.235	-.160	-1.097	.1393
Change in Divorce	-.160	-.161	-1.113	.1359
Change in Pct. Non-white	.130	.065	0.450	.3274
Change in females	.229	.143	0.880	.1918
R^2		.164		
Adj. R^2		.071		
Number of Observations		51		

Table 9.8   Effects of Change in Immigration on Change in Native Minority Unemployment, 1970 - 1980

Independent Variable	b	Beta	t-ratio	Prob.
Change in Immigration	.130	.248	1.645[b]	.0534
Change in Divorce	.004	.013	0.088	.4652
Change in Pct. Pop. under 25	-.029	-.105	-0.747	.2294
Change in Pct. Female	.094	.205	1.322[c]	.0965
Change in Unskilled Non-whites	.306	.256	1.771b	.0416
R^2		.155		
Adj. R^2		.061		
Number of Observations		51		

a Significant at $p < .01$ (one tailed test).
b Significant at $p < .05$ (one-tailed test).
c Significant at $p < .10$ (one-tailed test).

unemployment. These results hold even after taking into account the effects of a variable that has been consistently linked to minority unemployment, the percentage of unskilled minorities. The standardized regression coefficient (.25) shows that a one standard deviation unit change in immigration during that period brought about .25 standard deviation increase in minority unemployment levels. Findings in Table 9.8 also show increases in minority unemployment during the 1970-1980 period as a function of the percentage without skill. The latter was the strongest determinant of change in minority unemployment.

Metropolitan Level Results of the Effect of Immigration On Native Unemployment, 1980

Metropolitan level analysis on the effects of immigration on unemployment among natives as a whole, and minorities in particular are presented in Table 9.9. The equation in column 1 shows that immigrants had negative effects on native unemployment. The regression coefficient indicates that a one percentage increase in immigrants in an MSA led to a decrease of .354 in the percentage of natives without jobs, adjusting for the effects of the other variables in the equation. Column 2 indicates that percentage immigrants had no statistically significant impact on minority unemployment. However, the big difference between the coefficients in columns 1 and 2 appears to suggest that minorities do not derive benefits from whatever employment potentials exist as a consequence of immigration. The possibility exists that immigration does in fact increase minority unemployment.

Other variables in the equations warrant some comment. Percentage with less than high school education has a marginal, but statistically significant impact on native unemployment. The negative effect seems to imply that persons with less or no education probably go into low-paying jobs in secondary labor markets, and one possible effect of this is a reduction in the overall unemployment rate.

The most important determinant of unemployment for natives as a whole is work disability. The unstandardized regression coefficient for percentage with work disability is 1.575, indicating that a one-percentage increase in work disability increased the MSA unemployment rate by 1.575. A standard deviation unit increase in work disability led to a .644 standard deviation increase in native unemployment, controlling for the effects of other variables in equation 1. For minorities, however, work disability was unrelated to unemployment,

Table 9.9   Metropolitan Level Results of the Effects of Immigration on Native and Minority Unemployment, 1980

Independent Variables	Native Unemployment	Minority Unemployment
Percent Immigrants		
Std. estimate	-.354[a]	-.014
t-value	-.448	-.022
	-7.202	-.413
Percent with less than High School Education		
Std. estimate	-.079[c]	---
t-value	-.126	
	-1.429	
Percent Non-white		
Std. estimate	.044	---
t-value	.095	
	1.293	
Percent Females		
Std. estimate	.082	.052
t-values	.021	.017
	.343	.315
Average Age		
Std. estimate	-.314[c]	---
t-value	-.082	
	-1.319	
Percent with Work Disability		
Std. estimate	1.575[a]	.104
t-value	.644	.055
	8.744	.964
Percent Divorced		
Std. estimate	-.205[a]	.186[a]
t-value	-.190	.222
	-2.364	3.867

Table 9.9 Continued

Percent Minorities		
without Skills		
Std. estimate	---	.824
t-value		13.972
Percent under 25		
Std. estimate	---	-.037
t-value		
	-.719	
R^2	.852	.814
Adj. R^2	.840	.795
Number of Observations	76	76

2.005[a]

-.057

although the coefficient is positive.

Divorce seems to behave differently for natives as a whole and non-whites. When natives as a whole are considered, percentage divorced has a negative impact on native unemployment. The standardized estimate of the effect of divorce on native unemployment is -.205, indicating that a one-percentage increase in divorce led to a decrease in native unemployment by .205. A standard deviation increase in divorce reduced native unemployment rate by .190 standard deviation units. Divorce, however, increases the non-white unemployment rate. A one-percent increase in divorce led to an increase in non-white unemployment by .186 in 1980, taking into account the effects of other variables in the equation in column 2.

Non-white unemployment appears to be a function in part of lack of skill. A one percentage increase in minorities without skills increases the minority unemployment rate by 2%, controlling for the effects of other variables. In standardized units, a standard deviation unit increase in non-white low skill level increases non-white unemployment by .824 standard deviation units, taking into account other variables in the equation.

The equations in Table 9.9 were estimated on data from MSAs with immigrants 10% or more of the population. Results of this analysis are outlined in Appendix I.

For natives as a whole, immigration had a significant and negative impact on unemployment in 1980. The unstandardized coefficient of the effect of immigration on native unemployment is -.309, indicating that when other variables are controlled, a one percentage increase in immigration reduced native unemployment by .309. In standardized units, a standard deviation increase in immigration was associated with a decrease in native unemployment by .427 standard deviation units.

Results presented in column 2 show that immigration had no significant impact on non-white unemployment. Like before, the big difference in the coefficients for natives as a whole and minorities show that non-whites do not benefit from increases in immigration.

Whereas in Table 9.9 percentage non-white was unrelated to native unemployment, the equation in column 1 of Appendix I indicates that percentage non-whites increases native unemployment considerably. A one-percent increase in non-whites in an MSA with immigrant populations 10% or more increases native unemployment by nearly 21%. The foregoing result, contrasted with the negative effect of immigration imply that whereas the nation as a whole may benefit from increases in immigration, minorities may be hurt. Immigrants and minorities may be substitutes that are locked in competitive positions within the labor market.

Work disability exerts a strong positive influence on native unemployment. A one percentage increase in work disability increases native unemployment by nearly 2.32. In standard deviation units, a standard deviation increase in work disability increases native unemployment by .965 standard deviation units, controlling for the effects of other variables. For natives as a whole, percentage divorced had a negative impact on unemployment. Percentage females is unrelated to native unemployment, and average age increases native unemployment. The significant variables in equation 1 explained 93 percent of the variance in native unemployment.

Looking back at the equation in column 2, the only variable that reaches significance at the .05 level is the percentage of non-whites without skills. Percentage divorced is now only marginally related to minority unemployment. The adjusted R^2 drops from 84% in equation 2 of Table 9.9 to a little over 48% in equation 2 in Table I.1 (Appendix I).

Chapter 10

Immigration and Economic Dependence

The question of whether, and to what extent immigrants are economically dependent on public assistance income remains a subject of ongoing debate. Quite often, although arguments in this debate have not been based on empirical evidence, they have influenced legislation and public policy. The passage of Proposition 187 in California, and the recent Personal Responsibility Act passed by the U.S. Congress to a large extent assumed that immigrants use welfare disproportionately. This chapter provides an opportunity to fully investigate the degree to which foreign-born persons use transfer payments. Due to the nature of the problem, results presented are limited to individual level analysis. Furthermore, due to data limitations, only three panels will be studied. These include 1960, 1970, and 1980.

Economic dependence was measured by the variables, public assistance income, and Social Security income. Public assistance includes income from Aid to Families with Dependent Children (AFDC), old-age assistance, general assistance, aid to the blind, and aid to the permanently disabled (Supplementary Security Income). Although these payments can be received from the Federal government, some may come from State or local governments (U.S. Bureau of the Census, 1983a). In the 1960 census questionnaire, public assistance comprised income from: Social Security pensions, Veterans' payments, or any other source. Note then that Social Security was classified with other kinds of public assistance in 1960. Social Security income include survivors' benefits, permanent disability insurance payments, and special benefit payments made by the Social Security Administration. Government payments under the Railroad Retirement Act are also included in Social Security (U.S. Bureau of the Census, 1983a).

Effects of Immigrant Status on Public Assistance
Reception, 1960 to 1980

Table 10.1 presents findings on the effects on immigrant status on public assistance utilization, controlling for the effects of other variables. The findings show that immigrants were slightly more likely that natives to use public assistance in the 1950 to 1960 decade, but the difference between the two groups was only .034. In the 1960 to 1970 decade, immigrants also had a slightly higher probability (.004) of using public assistance than natives. In the 1970 to 1980 decade, however, immigrants were unlikely to use public assistance. These findings reveal some irony. The new immigration that is frequently associated with the utilization of public welfare did not begin until the 1970's. Therefore, if immigrants who came to the United States during the 1970's were more likely than natives to use public assistance, a positive relationship would be expected between immigrant status and public assistance utilization, and this should be reflected in the 1980 census. Yet positive effects between immigrant status and public assistance use were not observed in 1980, but in 1960 and 1970. In fact, in 1980, immigrants were less likely than natives to use public assistance.

Effects of other variables in Table 10.1 need some brief comments. In the 1950 to 1960 decade, regardless of national origin, non-whites were less likely than whites to use public assistance income. In the decades following, however, non-whites were more likely than natives to participate in public assistance, even when other factors like poverty and unemployment are taken into account. Age increased the likelihood of public assistance use in 1960 and 1980, but in 1970, age reduced the chances of public welfare dependence. Unmarried individuals were on average more likely to be on public assistance than married persons. This finding holds for all three decades under study. The largest difference or probability is found in 1980.

Except in the 1950 to 1960 decade, (reflected in the 1960 panel), higher educational levels reduced the chances of public assistance use. The positive coefficients observed between education and public assistance use in 1960 may be due to the inclusion of Social Security income within the former. Number of children under 18 in the

Independent Variable	1960	1970	1980
Immigrant Status	.034[a]	.004[a]	-.002
Std. estimate	.024	.012	-.003
t-ratio	7.620	3.244	-1.106
Weeks Worked	-.004[a]	.002[a]	-.004[a]
Std. estimate	-.032	.040	-.077
t-ratio	-5.713	9.007	-18.122
Race	-.035[a]	.017[a]	.035[a]
Std. estimate	-.027	.049	.064
t-ratio	-8.180	13.325	23.669
Age	.006[a]	-.000[a]	.001[a]
Std. estimate	.190	-.013	.074
t-ratio	54.375	-3.412	25.611
Marital Status	.099[a]	.016[a]	.069[a]
Std. estimate	.100	.063	.167
t-ratio	30.499	16.247	57.649
Education	.011[a]	-.000[a]	-.003[a]
Std. estimate	.087	-.014	-.049
t-ratio	25.596	-3.746	-17.648
Children under 18	.000	.005[a]	.014[a]
Std. estimate	.000	.065	.091
t-ratio	.065	17.072	32.605
Sex	-.138[a]	.011[a]	.007[a]
Std. estimate	-.166	.050	.018
t-ratio	-44.428	13.361	6.616
Unemployment	.008[c]	.034[a]	.036[a]
Std. estimate	.009	.100	.086
t-ratio	1.653	23.799	21.030

Table 10.1   Continued

Poverty	--	.020ᵃ	.105ᵃ
Std. estimate	--	.045	.163
t-ratio		11.850	57.986
Region	.004	-.006ᵃ	-.002ᶜ
Std. estimate	.004	-.024	-.005
t-ratio	1.390	-6.685	-1.919
R²	.063	.030	.130
Number of Observations	95,803	75,305	130,868

a significant at p < .01.
b significant at p < .05.
c significant at p < .10.
-- data unavailable in 1960.

household increased welfare dependence. This is not surprising, given the fact that one of the components of public assistance is AFDC. Except in 1960, females were more likely than men to receive public assistance.   Unemployment and poverty were among the strongest determinants of public assistance utilization in 1970 and 1980. In fact, in 1980, poverty was the single most important determinant of public assistance dependence. Those in poverty were nearly 10% more likely to be on public assistance than persons above poverty.

Logistic Regression Results of the Probability of Public Assistance Reception, 1980

Further analysis was performed, including additional variables in the equation. Variables added include alien status, work disability, public transportation disability, years since immigration, English proficiency, and unemployment. Analysis including these new variables are limited to the 1 percent (B) sample of the 1980 Census. Logistic regression estimation was performed on a 5% probability subsample. Of the 347,665 sampled individuals, a total subsample of 17,424 persons was obtained. Findings from the analysis are presented in Table 10.2. OLS equivalents are shown in Appendix J.

Results show that immigrant status has no significant effects on public assistance utilization, but the coefficient (b) is in the negative direction. In the OLS analysis, however, immigrants are significantly less likely to use public assistance relative to natives. Alien status has a significant negative impact on the odds of public assistance use. The logit coefficient of alien status (-.598) indicates that alien status reduces the log-odds of public assistance use by .598.

Interpretation of logit coefficients in terms of increases or decreases in log-odds resulting from a unit increase in a given predictor variable lacks much intuitive appeal. Additionally, most researchers seem more comfortable in talking in terms of probabilities of events occurring instead of odds. As a consequence, some analysts choose to transform logit coefficients into probabilities or slope coefficients. One widely used formula for converting logit coefficients into probabilities is the expression:

$$b(1-P)P \qquad\qquad (1)$$

where b is the computed logit coefficient; P is the sample mean of Y, the dependent variable (likelihood of the event occurring); and (1-P) is the

Table 10.2 Logistic Regression (ML) Results of the Probability of Public Assistance Reception, 1980

Independent Variable	b	b(1-P)P	Semi Std. coeff.	Semi Std. Δ in P(Y=1)	t-ratio
Immigrant Status	-.338	-.012	-.110	-.004	-1.088
Alien Status	-.598	-.027	-.150	-.005	-2.009
Education	-.086	-.003	-.279	-.009	-6.237
Marital Status	1.387	.050	.679	.034	13.250
Race	.459	.017	.187	.007	4.728
English Proficiency	-.139	-.005	-.103	-.004	-1.889
Work Disability	1.270	.046	.368	.016	10.430
Pub. Transp. Disab.	.806	.029	.111	.004	4.741
Weeks Worked in 1979	-.024	-.001	-.532	-.015	-7.147
Poverty	1.023	.037	.322	.014	10.420
Years Since Immigr.	.039	.001	.021	.001	.276
Region	.181	.007	.089	.004	1.928
Age	.016	.001	.228	.010	4.416
Children under 18	.785	.029	.392	.017	7.373
Sex	.819	.030	.409	.018	8.064
Unemployment	.444	.016	.209	.008	3.310
Constant	-4.368				

Log Likelihood = -1987.43.
Degrees of freedom = 16.
Pseudo R^2 = .085.

Likelihood Ratio Statistic = 1627.71.
Sample mean of Y = .038.
Number of Observations: 17,424

difference between 1 and the sample mean (likelihood of failure). Each computed coefficient is simply multiplied by results from $(1-P)P$ (see, for example, Morgan and Teachman, 1988: 932; Portes, 1984:391; Rexroat and Shehan, 1984: 353). However, since the logistic curve is nonlinear, coefficients derived are very sensitive to the value of P, and tend to change as the latter changes along various points of the curve.

Petersen (1985:130) argues that when a given independent variable is continuous, the interpretation of a coefficient derived from the above formula is simple, but when a predictor is categorical, the formula presents a slope of the dependent variable for an infinitesimal change in a categorical variable, an outcome that does not make sense. Petersen (1985:131) recommends an alternative formula for calculating the change in the probability resulting from a unit change in an independent variable (both categorical or continuous):

$$\Delta P = P(=1|L_1) - P(D=1|L_o)$$
$$= \exp (L_1) / [1 + \exp(L_1)]$$
$$- \exp (L_o) / [1 + \exp(L_o)] \qquad (2)$$

where L_o is the logit coefficient before the unit change in a given independent variable, and $L_1 = L_o + b_x$ is the logit after the unit change in the independent variable (x). Estimated coefficients represent changes in probabilities resulting from unit changes in the respective predictor variables.

Column 4 of Table 10.2 presents results based on a derivative of Petersen's formula. Whereas the latter presents logit coefficients in their unstandardized form, column 4 is an attempt at standardization. The formula used to derive the entries in column 4 is:

$$SS\Delta P = 1/1 + e^{-L}{}_1 - 1/1 + e^{-L}{}_0 \qquad (3)$$

where: $SS\Delta P$ is interpreted as the change in probability of the dependent variable for a one standard deviation change in a given model covariate. $L_o = \ln P/1-P$, and $L_1 = L_o + bS_x$. Ln is the natural logarithm and S_x is the standard deviation of x. bS_x is the semi standardized coefficient of b (the logit coefficient). Thus, the only difference between (2) and (3) is that in the latter, the semi standardized estimate is used instead of the unstandardized (b). Computed   coefficients may be interpreted as changes in probability of the dependent variable for a one   standard deviation change in an independent variable with the former evaluated at its mean (Kposowa, 1987b:6; 1995).

In column 4, the semi-standardized change in probability of public assistance use for alien status is -.005. It means that evaluated at the sample mean (.038), a one standard deviation change in alien status is associated with a .005 decrease in the probability of using public assistance. In unstandardized units, the difference between aliens and citizens is -.598 of the odds of receiving public assistance.

A few other results in Table 10.2 are examined in the next couple of paragraphs. Education decreases the probability of receiving public assistance. Persons that are unmarried (marital status) are more likely to use public assistance than the married. The difference between the married and unmarried is 1.387 of the odds of receiving public assistance. Work disability and public transportation disability significantly increase the probability of being on public assistance. Likewise, being in poverty increases the chances of public assistance dependence. Females are significantly more likely than men to be on public assistance. Presence of children under 18 in a household increases the chances of public assistance dependence. The number of years since immigration appears unrelated to public assistance reliance in the logistic model, but it increases public assistance use in the OLS model (Appendix J).

Semi-standardized coefficients which assess the relative importance of the independent variables are presented in column 3 of Table 10.2. A review of these coefficients show that the strongest determinant of public assistance use in 1980 was being unmarried (.679). This was followed by number of weeks worked (-.532); being female (.409); presence of children under 18 in a household (.392); work disability (.368), and poverty (.322).

The likelihood ratio statistic (ls) was computed by the formula:

$$LS = -2(\ln L_{ull} - \ln L_{model}) \tag{4}$$

where L_{ull} is the sample likelihood when there is no effect of the independent variables. That is, $\beta_1 = \beta_2 = \beta_3 = 0$. In this case, the probability of the dependent variable is a constant, and does not change with the independent variables. The formula for the L_{ull} is given below.

$$L_{ull} = N_1 \ln(N_1/N_1 + N_2) + N_2 \ln(N_2/N_1 + N_2) \tag{5}$$

L_{model} was obtained from a BMDP printout. The LS for the model as a whole is 1627.71. With 16 degrees of freedom, the latter shows that we must reject the hypothesis of no effects of the independent variables, and conclude that the set of independent variables predict the log likelihood of public assistance use.

Results show that immigrants and aliens were much less likely than natives to be on public assistance income. These results imply that fears of disproportionate numbers of post 1970 immigrants being on public welfare may be groundless. The evidence shows otherwise. The concerns may be based on faulty assumptions, especially when it is applied to illegal aliens. Persons who enter the United States illegally are afraid of coming into contact with government officials out of fear of deportation. In the light of this, they are unlikely to apply for public welfare assistance, since the process could bring them into contact with the government.

Effects of Immigrant Status on Social Security Reception, 1970 to 1980

In a sense, Social Security is not strictly speaking economic dependence. It is a "pay as you go" retirement (trust) fund. However, to the extent that the system is in part financed by persons currently in the labor force, it could be used as an indicator of an economic 'burden', carried by present workers. Therefore, from a policy point of view, it may be important to know the extent to which immigrants depend on this sort of income. Table 10.3 presents findings for the effects of immigrant status on Social Security utilization. Note that 1960 figures are not given. This is because Social Security data for 1960 were classified as public assistance, and they were included in the analysis presented in Table 10.1.

Results show that immigrants were much less likely than natives to be on Social Security, and this holds true for both decades, 1960 and 1970 (as reflected in the 1970 panel), and 1970 to 1980 (as seen in the 1980 panel). In 1980, immigrants were even much less likely than natives to be on Social Security. Findings are in some respects similar to those observed with regard to public assistance use with some exceptions. Non-whites were significantly less likely than whites to be on Social Security in 1980.

Women were significantly more likely than men to be on Social Security in the 1960 to 1970 decade, but they were much less likely to be on it in 1980. Unmarried persons are significantly more likely than the

Table 10.3   Determinants of Social Security Dependence, 1970 - 1980

Independent Variable	1960			1980		
	b	Beta	t	b	Beta	t
Immigrant Status	-.010	-.022	-6.185	-.038	-.044	-17.046
Weeks Worked	-.010	-.131	-34.765	-.014	-.216	-52.957
Children under 18	.000	.010	2.624	-.011	-.060	-21.992
Education	-.000	-.021	-5.643	-.004	-.054	-20.072
Race	-.002	-.004	-1.171	-.008	-.013	-5.001
Marital Status	.027	.086	22.491	.056	.118	42.105
Sex	.006	.002	5.964	-.036	-.080	-29.622
Age	.001	.141	36.104	.004	.232	82.171
Region	.006	.021	5.799	-.011	-.024	-9.222
R^2	.040			.160		
Number of Observations	75,305			130,868		

married to be on Social Security, and this was especially true in 1980. Age significantly increases the probability of Social Security dependence. Higher educational levels decrease the likelihood of dependence on Social Security. The coefficients of determination in all the equations are relatively small. However, in using categorical dependent variables as done here, focus is not on percent of variance explained, but rather on the magnitude and direction of the effects of independent variables.

Logistic Regression Results of the Probability of Social Security Reception, 1980

Table 10.4 presents findings on the determinants of Social Security dependence with additional variables controlled. Variables added to the equation include alien status (aliens), years since immigration, English proficiency, work disability, public transportation disability, poverty, and unemployment. Comparable OLS estimates are presented in Appendix K.   Immigrants were significantly less likely than natives to be on Social Security. The logit coefficient (b) of the odds of the dependent variable for immigrant status is -.611. It indicates that the difference between immigrants and natives was -.611 of receiving Social Security income. Alien status had no significant effects on the probability of being on Social Security, but the coefficients were in the expected negative direction, suggesting that aliens were unlikely to be on Social Security.   Possible reasons for this have already been alluded to, including fear of contact with government officials. Age may also be a factor if aliens are on average younger than citizens. Understandably, the probability of Social Security use may increase with duration of residence in the United States, but the probability seems low.

With regard to the relative importance of other variables in the model in Table 10.4, it is necessary to examine the semi standardized coefficients. Perhaps not surprisingly, although analysis was limited to persons between the ages of 16 and 64, age is the most important predictor of Social Security use. The semi standardized coefficient of age is .960, indicating that a change in the log-odds of being on Social Security is associated with a .96 standard deviation increase in age. Next in rank of importance were the number of weeks worked (-.887), and marital status (.510). Presumably, unmarried persons were much more likely to be on Social Security income than the married. Work disability was a strong predictor of Social Security dependence. Non-whites were significantly less likely than whites to use Social Security. The difference

Table 10.4   Logistic Regression (ML) Results of the Probability of Social Security Reception, 1980

Independent Variable	b	b(1-P)P	Semi Std. coeff.	Semi Std. Δ in P(Y=1)	t-ratio
Immigrant Status	-.611	-.031	-.199	-.023	-1.727
Alien Status	-.321	-.051	-.081	-.004	-0.976
Education	-.031	-.002	-.102	-.005	-2.635
Marital Status	1.042	.053	.510	.033	11.580
Race	-.244	-.012	-.099	-.005	-2.222
English Proficiency	.058	.003	.043	.002	0.752
Work Disability	.795	.405	.230	.013	8.270
Public Transportation Disability	.489	.025	.067	.004	3.250
Weeks Worked in 1979	-.040	-.002	-.887	-.031	-13.210
Poverty	-.470	-.024	-.148	-.007	-3.972
Years Since Immigration	.021	.001	.112	.006	1.661
Region	-.136	-.007	-.067	-.003	-1.695
Age	.069	.004	.960	.076	20.070
Children under 18	-.077	-.004	-.039	-.002	-0.776
Sex	-.497	-.025	-.248	-.011	-6.006
Unemployment	.471	.024	.221	.012	3.625
Constant	-5.093				

Log Likelihood = -2502.61.
Degrees of freedom = 16.
Pseudo R² = .117

Likelihood Ratio Statistic = 2300.75
Sample mean of Y = .054
Number of observations = 17,424

between the two races (whites and non-whites) was .244 of the odds of being on Social Security. Women were significantly less likely than men to be on Social Security. Presence of children under 18 was unrelated to being on Social Security. The Likelihood Ratio Statistic (LS) for the whole model is 2300.75. It indicates that the hypothesis of no effects of the independent variables must be rejected, in favor of a an alternative conclusion that the set of independent variables predict the likelihood of Social Security reception.

Chapter 11

Discussion and Conclusions

This study set out initially to investigate the effects of immigration on the United States economy. Specific aspects of the economy considered were native earnings, native socioeconomic attainment, native occupational prestige, native industrial sector (segmentation), native unemployment, and immigrant economic dependence. A trend, as opposed to a one shot cross-sectional design was adopted as a working research design for testing various hypotheses. Human capital, dual labor market, and equilibrium theories provided the theoretical framework, and the units of analysis were individuals (1940 to 1980), states (1940 to 1980), and Metropolitan Statistical Areas (1980).

The present chapter is divided into three sections. First, discussions and conclusions focus on immigrant status. In short, the issue under discussion is whether immigrant status exerts unique effects on the dependent variables after adjusting for the effects of human capital variables. Second, results of the various hypotheses on the impacts of immigration on the general native population as a whole are discussed. Finally, the effects of immigration on minorities (non-whites) are summarized and reviewed.

Impact of Immigrant and Alien status

Human capital theorists argue that each individual derives earnings based upon skills which he or she brings to the labor market. These skills can be measured by schooling and job experience. The theory assumes that other personal characteristics are irrelevant in the job

162

Chapter Eleven

market. In view of this, it was predicted that immigrant status (a non-human capital characteristic) would have no unique effects on earnings. Evidence from the analysis provided only partial support for this hypothesis. Immigrants earned significantly more than natives in 1940 and 1950. In 1940, the difference between immigrants and natives in terms of earnings was $151.73 in favor of immigrants. In 1950, the difference still favored immigrants, but it had decreased to $105.87. In both decades, the differences between the two groups were statistically significant. In 1960, natives earned on average $24.33 more than immigrants. By 1970, the difference had increased to $32.56 in favor of natives, but in 1980, natives earned on average only $0.73 more than immigrants. The 1960, 1970, and 1980 results were statistically insignificant, although immigrants earned slightly less than natives, as reflected in the negative coefficients observed during those decades.

Findings in the descriptive statistics appeared to suggest that immigrants have traditionally had less human capital than the native born in terms of years of school completed, especially in the 1970s. Multivariate analysis indicated, however, that these differences in human capital have not translated into unusually sharp disparities in earnings as has been suggested in past literature. Findings imply that immigrant status itself is not indicative of low earnings. The most important determinants of earnings are such human capital variables as education and age. Once these are controlled, immigrant status is not a strong predictor of earnings. For immigrants, earnings increase the longer they have been in the United States. Presumably, this occurs because they increase their American labor market experience.

While the difference between immigrants and natives in earnings was small and only marginally significant in 1980, the case for aliens was different. Alien status was used in the analysis as a crude proxy for illegal aliens. Findings showed that in 1980, aliens earned significantly less than citizens. The difference between aliens and citizens in earnings was $377.13. Reasons for this are widely discussed in the literature. Not only might aliens have lower human capital levels than citizens, but their illegal nature implies that frequently they do not have much bargaining power in terms of negotiating for higher earnings. Employers pay them whatever the former consider adequate. Furthermore, since aliens are in secondary labor markets, they have less job stability. They change jobs frequently, and in the process they establish an unstable job history with accompanying lower wages.

Human capital theory's main thrust is an explanation of earnings. The present study argued, however, that the theory can be used to explain individual differences in socioeconomic attainment and occupational prestige. The rationale for this was based on the assumption that these variables are strongly tied to earnings. The higher the prestige of a job held by an individual, the higher his or her earnings, and the higher the earnings, the higher his or her socioeconomic attainment and vice versa. In general, individuals would opt to be socially mobile, and to achieve higher status. Since human capital theory explains earnings as a function of individual skills and experience, it was predicted that likewise, socioeconomic attainment and occupational prestige would be determined by skills and experience.

Accordingly, hypothesis 2 stated that immigrant status will have no unique effects on socioeconomic attainment and prestige. Evidence from the analysis provided only partial support for this hypothesis. The human capital variables, education and age had strong effects on occupational prestige and socioeconomic attainment. At the same time, immigrant status had significant negative effects on prestige in 1960, and no effects in 1970.

In 1980, immigrant status was found to have a positive impact on socioeconomic status. One implication of this is that in the decade prior to 1980, immigrants were significantly likely to have achieved higher status occupations. However, the distance between immigrants and natives in terms of occupational attainment was only .01 standard deviation units in favor of immigrants.

Results further show that the socioeconomic attainment of immigrants is initially high, but it may deteriorate the longer they are in the United States, implying that perhaps the longer immigrants are in the United States, the more they become like natives.

In one respect, the 1980 findings present a puzzle. The descriptive statistics and previous research show that human capital levels of post 1970 immigrants are lower than those of Americans. One might thus, have expected that immigrants would have lower SES than natives, but analysis provides contrary evidence. Moreover, even after adjusting for the effects of human capital variables, immigrant status influenced SES. An alternative explanation to human capital has to be found.

One possibility is that socioeconomic status scores used on 1980 data measure something completely different from what is measured by prestige scores. It is, however, quite unlikely that measurement problems alone account for the differences in signs of immigrant status and prestige (1960 and 1970), and immigrant status and SES (1980). Prestige and socioeconomic status scores are known to be highly correlated (Treiman, 1977:210). Reasons for the apparent inconsistencies will be explored in future research. A starting point would be to use prestige scores as the dependent variable in all three panels, and then use SES scores as the dependent variable on the same panels. Whatever the outcome of such a study, present results imply that a significant number of immigrants have achieved economic success in the United States.

Dual labor market theory assumes that there are institutional constraints that prevent free movement between primary and secondary labor market sectors. Discrimination is one such impediment, and tends to confine minorities and immigrants, especially recently arrived ones to the secondary labor market sector. It was thus decided to test the thesis that immigrants are in secondary labor markets. Accordingly, hypothesis 3 predicted that immigrant status would have significant negative effects on industrial sector. In other words, it was expected that immigrants will be more likely to tend towards secondary labor markets as opposed to core or primary markets. Evidence found in the analysis is in general support of hypothesis 3. Both immigrants and aliens appear to be absent from core and oligopolistic industries, and sectors decrease with immigrant or alien status. The result is consistent across the three time panels studied, 1960 through 1980. Results show that the tendency of immigrants to be absent from core and oligopolistic industries was strongest in 1970, but it weakened in 1980. Perhaps this weakening in their presence away from core industries in part explains the slight gains made by immigrants in socioeconomic attainment noted above.

Minorities also appear to have been absent from core and oligopolistic industries in 1960 and 1970, but they made some gains towards entering these industries in 1980. One implication of these results is that to the extent that both groups were in secondary labor markets, and to the extent that the two are generally substitutes for each other in production, immigrants may have competed with minorities in secondary labor markets in 1960 and 1970. However, this competition was less intense in 1980. While immigrants and aliens were still in secondary labor markets in 1980, at least some minorities seemed to be making some progress away from such markets in 1980. In general, the above results provide strong support for dual labor market theory.

Hypothesis 4 predicted that immigrant status will have no effects on unemployment. This hypothesis was based on a human capital assumption that in the labor market, jobs are abundant and freely available to anyone with proper skills. It was thus expected that the only determinants of unemployment would be the absence of such skills.

Data analysis shows that immigrants consistently appear to have suffered from higher unemployment than natives in every year studied, except 1950. The difference between immigrants and natives in terms of unemployment was widest in 1960. Analysis also shows that unemployment levels among immigrants decrease the longer they have been in the United States. In fact, logistic regression on data for 1980 suggested that when factors such as work disability and public transportation disability are controlled, there are no statistically significant differences between immigrants and natives in unemployment. As assumed by human capital theory, lack of skills (education) promotes unemployment. At the same time, other factors, such as race, sex, and immigrant status strongly increase an individual's chances being unemployed.

Immigrants and Economic Dependence

Economic dependence was indicated by the variables public assistance reliance, and Social Security income reception. Hypothesis 5 predicted that immigrant status will have no effects on public assistance use. Data reveal some inconsistencies. In 1960, immigrants were more likely to use public assistance than natives. In 1970, immigrants were also slightly more likely than natives to depend on public assistance. However, the difference between the two groups was extremely small, and it narrowed between 1960 and 1970. In 1980, immigrants and aliens were less likely than natives to receive public assistance. Duration of residence in the United States appears to increase the probability of public assistance use.

A number of conclusions can be drawn from the above findings. Most of the debates about the dependence of immigrants on American tax payers and public coffers have centered in recent years on post 1970 entrants. These are the ones whose skill levels have been found to be lower, and who are consequently believed to be unable to support themselves, and who end up being dependent on 'welfare' and other government assistance programs. Yet the data reveal some irony. It was immigrants who arrived prior to 1970 that were more likely to be dependent on American public tax payers. Post 1970 immigrants whose presence should be evident most in analysis for 1980 were less likely than natives to be on public welfare assistance. The data thus reveal that current fears about immigrants' use of public assistance may be unfounded.

Analysis of the determinants of public assistance use offer only partial support for human capital theory. Education reduces the likelihood of public assistance dependence. The coefficient was positive in 1960, but the explanation for this was the inclusion of Social Security income among public assistance income that year. Age, one of the human capital variables, reduced the chances of public assistance income in 1970. Among lessons to learn from the findings is that various factors increase the probability of public assistance dependence, some of which are not under the control of an individual. These include unemployment, poverty, and work disability.

Apart from the perception that immigrants take away jobs from native born Americans, one of the reasons for the resurgence of anti-foreign sentiments in the United States in recent years is the belief that immigrants, especially illegal aliens use transfer income. Analysis of data have shown that the facts are time dependent. In 1960 and 1970, immigrants were more likely to be economically dependent, relative to natives, but in 1980, they were less dependent. Aliens (being in illegal status) are generally afraid of deportation. They resist coming into contact with government officials because of such fears. As a result, it is unlikely that they would use public assistance financed by American tax payers, since the process ultimately entails completing documents and undergoing interviews that might reveal their status. The views expressed above are supported in the analysis by the negative coefficients found between alien status and public assistance use.

The foregoing statements about immigrants and public assistance need to be qualified. Immigrants in 1980 did not use public assistance financed by American tax payers any more than natives. This is not to suggest, however, that immigrants were not dependent in anyway. There are various other forms or channels of assistance in the United States that are not directly financed by tax payers. There are churches, non-profit organizations, and various other charity organizations that provide assistance, or are known to have helped immigrants, especially refugees. The extent and magnitude of such assistance is unknown. Furthermore, to the best knowledge of this author, there are no reliable data that might enable one to undertake a study of immigrant reliance on charities.

It could be that various immigrant subgroups use public assistance more than others and natives. Refugees are presumably one such group. Refugees fleeing their own countries may frequently require assistance until such a time as they are able to acquire skills that enable them to function independently in their new country. It makes sense to argue that such individuals may use welfare and other forms of government assistance on a temporary basis. Suggested here is that researchers interested in studying the reliance of immigrants on public assistance should in future carefully make distinctions between refugees and other immigrants. A sound beginning is to look for ways to collect reliable quantitative data.

A very important conclusion from the analysis is that variegated social ills and discrimination perpetrated against various disadvantaged groups in American society may be the real reasons for the use of public assistance. Factors such as poverty, work disability, unemployment, lack of education, racial intolerance, and to some extent a breakdown in the nuclear family are impediments that seem to drive people towards public assistance use. Immigrants are unwitting scapegoats, blamed because of their visibility. Scapegoating on the part of the public shifts attention away from the true causes of public assistance use that may be deeply tied to a more serious and potentially explosive problem of inequality and social injustice.

No hypothesis was specified with regard to immigrant dependence on Social Security income. Results in the analysis, however, found that in 1970, immigrants were significantly less likely than natives to receive Social Security income. In 1980, the difference between the two groups increased slightly. Results indicate that there are several other factors responsible for Social Security dependence. Of these, age is understandably the single most important factor. For immigrants, this is evident in the fact that the likelihood of Social Security use increases as residence in the United States increases. Obviously, immigrants become older the longer they are in the United States, and as a consequence, they may need Social Security.

The above comments about immigrant reliance on Social Security income also need to be qualified. It may be seriously inaccurate to infer from these findings that globally (internationally), immigrants are less likely to be on Social Security income than Americans (native born). Social Security is a retirement (pension) system. Thousands of immigrants in the United States work at jobs that guarantee reception of Social Security income upon retirement. It follows that if these immigrants work in the United States and retire, they would be eligible for Social Security. Some immigrants may, however, decide to return to their home (original) countries upon retirement. If they do return home, they will be absent from the U.S. census, even though they may in fact be receiving Social Security checks. In view of this, census data may be seriously inadequate for studying immigrant use of Social Security income. It was in recognition of the conceptual and data problems involved that no hypothesis was specified in connection with Social Security. There is the related conceptual problem of determining whether former immigrants who return to their home countries are still immigrants.

Effects of Immigration on the General Population

A fundamental question asked at the beginning of this book was: Does immigration benefit or hurt the United States? Part of this question has already been answered with regard to economic dependence. It was found and argued that immigrants and aliens are not economically dependent on U.S. tax payers. The third section of this chapter takes a more detailed review of findings on the impact of immigration on American society. Themes covered include the effects of immigration on native earnings, native socioeconomic attainment, native occupational prestige, native industrial sector, and native unemployment.

Hypothesis 6 anticipated that immigration would exert significant negative effects on native earnings. This hypothesis was based in part on human capital theory's assumption that employers would hire workers on the basis of human capital characteristics. Under the assumption that immigrants might have had higher levels of human capital in some periods of American history than natives, it was expected that employers might have favored immigrants over natives. A probable outcome of such a practice would have been competition between immigrants and natives.

Evidence from the analysis reveal that for every year studied, except 1940, immigrants had positive and significant effects on the earnings of the native born population. These results remained even after controlling for such human capital factors as education and age.

The findings failed to support human capital theory, except in 1940 when the predicted negative effect was found. Immigrants in 1940 appear to have had high skill levels. They may thus have been strong competitors with natives in the labor market. An outcome of that competition was a reduction in native earnings.

Dual labor market theory represents an alternative and more plausible explanation for the positive results found in other years. Suggested is that immigrant exploitation is a gain for natives. Immigrants take jobs that pay less, thereby contributing to economic growth. In the process natives take up higher paying jobs that bring them higher earnings. Employers hire immigrants not because the latter possess higher human capital than natives, but solely to increase their margin of profit. Since immigrants are generally willing to accept below minimum wages, employers can keep labor costs low. Since labor can be an expensive commodity in the United States, reduced spending on it ensures lower costs of producing goods and services. Low production costs in turn lead to higher returns on investment. Higher returns on investment might lead to economic expansion, and economic growth in turn leads to higher earnings for natives.

Results show that in areas with above average concentrations of immigrants, while the latter still exert an upward pressure on native earnings, there is a weakening in effects. These findings suggest that although immigration tends to bring about increases in native earnings, such increments tend to be minimal in areas with heavier concentrations of immigrants. Findings further indicate that the positive influences of immigration have generally declined with time. They were strongest in 1960. For the whole country at that time, a 1 percentage increase in the supply of immigrants brought about on average a 39 percent increase in native earnings. In 1980, however, a 1 percentage increment in immigration led to only an increase in native earnings of 27% on average. For the country as a whole, immigration was consistently the strongest predictor of native earnings from 1960, except in 1980 when it was replaced by college education. The same pattern was repeated in states with above average immigrant populations.

The consistency of results found in this study cast some doubts on findings in some past research that immigrants as a group depress native earnings. Results imply that immigration may to some extent constitute an economic asset to the United States. If immigrants were a burden on American society, then negative results would have been obtained in the regression coefficients. Yet positive effects were found for every year studied, except 1940. Ironically, 1940 was over two decades before the new immigration that led to the influx of large numbers of low skilled persons from third world countries. Borjas (1986:65) reported that immigrants have had a small negative effect on the earnings of white

native men. The present study finds no support for Borjas' conclusion.
Similarly, Matta and Popp's (1988:115) finding of a negative coefficient
between recently arrived immigrants and native earnings is not supported
here. If there are negative effects of post 1968 immigrants on native
earnings, then these should have been evident in equations on 1970 and
1980 data. Analysis, however, shows positive coefficients in both 1970
and 1980.

Hypothesis 7 predicted that immigrants will have negative effects
on native socioeconomic attainment and occupational prestige. The
rationale for this was the same as that for hypothesis 6. No support was
found for this hypothesis. Data reveal that in 1970, immigrants had a
significant and positive influence on native occupational prestige. In
1980, immigrants also exerted a significant and positive impact on native
socioeconomic status. Data show no impact on native prestige in 1960.
The upward pressure on native socioeconomic status coming from
immigrants in 1980 appears to have been strongest in metropolitan areas.
Although they weakened slightly, the positive impacts of immigrants on
native socioeconomic status remained even after concentrating on
immigrant enclaves, that is Metropolitan Statistical Areas with
immigrant populations 10% or more.

At the individual level, it was found that in 1980, immigrants
tended to have higher socioeconomic attainment than the native born. In
view of this, an alternative explanation (as opposed to human capital
explanations), has to be given for the positive influence of immigrants
on native socioeconomic attainment. It could be that as immigrants go
into higher socioeconomic status jobs, natives are forced, so to speak, to
compete with them or aim at even higher status jobs. As this process
unfolds, natives in turn raise their own socioeconomic attainment.
Immigrants may thus, promote occupational mobility among native
workers.

Hypothesis 8 predicted that immigration would lead to increases
in unemployment levels among natives. The rationale for this
hypothesis was derived from human capital theory, and it was based on
the assumption that if immigrants in some decades had had higher
human capital than natives, the two groups would have been engaged in
direct competition. Competition would have led to job loss among some
natives. Consequently, increases in immigration would have led to
corresponding increases in the native unemployment rate.

Data analysis failed to support human capital theory, and they
instead provide strong support for dual labor market theory. One of the

most consistent findings in the study is that immigration has negative impacts on unemployment among the native born population as a whole. These findings hold true even after we focus on only immigrant enclaves. How interpret these results? There are at least two possibilities.

Immigrants invest in the United States, and their investments lead to economic expansion. Economic opportunities are created, and these in turn lead to the creation of lots of jobs. Natives are employed as a consequence, and so native unemployment rates are reduced because of immigration. Another possibility is that immigrants take lower paying jobs or jobs that natives despise. In the process, they push up natives into higher paying jobs. The overall effect is an increase in job opportunities as the economy adjusts to create niches to accommodate natives in higher paying occupations. The ultimate consequence is an increase in employment, and a concomitant decrease in unemployment.

Either of the above possibilities may be correct, but the second is more probable. Many immigrants coming to the United States may invest in terms of their human capital and other skills, but it is unlikely that most have sufficient amount of capital to invest on such a large scale, as to make significant impacts on unemployment at the national level. On the other hand, if above average numbers of immigrants take up jobs at the lower end of the economic spectrum (in the secondary labor market), their presence may have considerable positive effects on the overall national economy.

In hypothesis 9, it was predicted that immigration would have significant positive effects on native industrial sector. This hypothesis was derived from an assumption in dual labor market theory that a competitive/substitutability relationship exists between immigrants and minorities in the secondary labor market. Accordingly, it was expected that as competition between minorities and immigrants increased, the beneficiaries would be the native majority.

It has already been shown at the micro level that a substantial number of immigrants tend to be located in the secondary sector of the labor market. Since large numbers of natives, especially minorities are also in this market, it is reasonable to assume that a certain degree of competition will take place between the two groups. The present hypothesis sought to determine the impacts this competition might have on the sectors in the labor market in which natives would be present. In short, the question being asked is: are natives pushed up or down the industrial hierarchy by immigrants? As a corollary, are natives better off or worse off in industry as a consequence of immigration?

In 1960 and 1970, evidence from the analysis provided strong support for dual labor market theory, and for hypothesis 9. At the state level, and in the whole country, immigrants seemed to push up natives towards core and oligopolistic industries. The strongest push was in 1970. Non-whites were absent from oligopolistic industries, as evident by the observed negative coefficients. This lends partial support to the competition thesis. When we focus on states with immigrant populations in excess of 5% of the population, immigrants still pushed up natives but only in 1960 and 1970. In 1980, they seemed to exert a down ward pressure on natives in industry, although this effect was insignificant.

How to explain the insignificant negative 1980 results? It is highly likely that the 1980 results are a consequence of American industrial problems in the 1970s. It has been mentioned elsewhere that high unemployment and a recession hit the U.S. economy in the 1970s. Low industrial output, low productivity, and reduced profits by American industry probably meant less upward mobility for workers, regardless of national origin. These observations again lead to a point already made in this book that the impacts of immigration on American society depends to some extent on the health of the U.S. economy. During times of prosperity, like in the 1960s, immigrants make positive contributions, but in times of economic difficulties, such effects are either absent or negative.

Equilibrium theorists hold that migration is in response to imbalances in regional development. Accordingly, migration tends to be from areas of low wages to areas of high wages. Applied to immigration, the theory predicts that immigrants are drawn to regions of the host country that have stronger economies and that, therefore, offer higher wages and promises better opportunities. The theory thus anticipates a positive relationship between immigration and regional expansion. Analysis (not presented) showed that immigration in 1970 was positively related to economic expansion in 1970 (r=.253), and economic expansion in 1970 was positively related to subsequent immigration in 1980 (r=.436). Economic expansion in 1980 was positively related to immigration in 1980 (r=.295). The patterns of these correlations (especially between economic expansion in 1970 and immigration in 1980) suggest that immigrants may in part be drawn to states with expanding economies.

To avoid drawing spurious conclusions, it was predicted (hypothesis 10) that once economic expansion is controlled, immigration will have no significant effects on American earnings. No support was found for this hypothesis. Analysis showed that even after controlling for economic growth, immigrants continued to have positive effects on native earnings. Results imply that the relationship between immigration and native earnings is not spurious. The observed positive effects of immigrants on native earnings are not due to mere regional growth patterns.

Effects of Immigration on Native Minorities

Although on average immigration appears to benefit the American population as a whole, results have shown that subgroups within the society, for example, minorities, are hurt by immigration. Findings on the effects of immigration on the native population as a whole on one hand, and minorities on the other, support two sociological perspectives. One perspective views immigration as functional for society, and argues that immigration does not harm the American labor market. It regards immigrants as performing complementary roles beside natives. Accordingly, the labor market is not fixed, but it is constantly expanding. There are enough pieces of the pie, so to speak, to go around for everybody, both immigrants and natives.

The foregoing argument is often proposed by those who favor the functionalist perspective of immigration. Immigrants are seen as performing tasks that natives do not want. Presumably, in the absence of immigration, such jobs will go unperformed as there are few natives willing to take them. Results from this study generally support the functionalist perspective of immigration. However, analysis shows that this perspective holds true for only the majority. Immigrants appear to increase the occupational mobility and earnings of the white majority, but their negative impacts on minorities should not be underestimated.

Findings have shown that for minorities, another sociological framework, the conflict perspective is what best explains the impact of immigration. Immigrants compete with minorities in the secondary labor market for jobs. The competition between the two groups leads to job loss and reduced earnings for minorities.

Hypothesis 11 predicted that the higher the level of immigration, the higher the native minority unemployment rate. The rationale for this hypothesis is strongly rooted in dual labor market theory. Competition between immigrants and minorities in the secondary labor market may lead to job loss for minorities, especially in places where employers are racially insensitive to non-whites, and their sole agenda is to maximize profits, while minimizing labor costs.   In   such an environment, immigrants (willing to accept lower wages) might be preferred by employers over minorities. Higher minority unemployment rates may thus, result. Findings from the analysis support dual labor market theory and hypothesis 11. Immigration in 1970 and 1980 had direct increasing effects on non-white minority unemployment, even after taking minority skill levels into account. Furthermore, increases in unemployment rates among non-whites between 1970 and 1980 were directly linked to corresponding increases in the immigration rate between the two periods.

Immigrants seem to be substitutes with those at the lower end of the economy. Although immigrants may perhaps improve upon their human capital over time in the United States, this research suggests that a lot seem to begin their U.S. employment experience in jobs located in the peripheral sector of the economy. This may happen on account of many reasons. One is the simple fact that they lack enough knowledge about their new country for them to take full advantage of whatever opportunities exist. Second, unless they initially entered the United States with high skills or as students who subsequently became skilled, immigrants are likely to settle in areas already inhabited by previous immigrants. If the latter are still in secondary labor market jobs, the new entrants are likely to begin there themselves. It is not uncommon for past immigrants to help new immigrants settle down and get adjusted to their new country. They may eventually move away from there as they acquire more human capital in terms of education and job experience. In the meantime, however, their presence in the peripheral sector brings them into conflict with minorities for jobs in secondary labor market.

In accordance with dual labor market theory which posits competition between minorities and immigrants in the secondary sector, hypothesis 12 predicted that the higher the level of immigration, the lower the earnings of native minorities. This hypothesis was tested for only 1980, since the preceding decade had witnessed inflows of unprecedented numbers of immigrants from Southeast Asia and Latin America. These immigrants are believed to have had lower skill levels, and they are, therefore, strong competitors and substitutes for minorities in production. Evidence from the analysis strongly supports hypothesis 12. Immigration has direct negative effects on minority earnings, even after adjusting for human capital variables and minority skill levels.

Two possible explanations may be offered for this finding. First, immigrants and minorities fight for scarce jobs in the secondary labor market. Since there is abundant supply of labor, and supply exceeds demand, employers have no incentive to raise wages. As a result, general wage levels in a given metropolitan area remain low, so minority earnings are low. Another explanation is that in some cases or some localities, employers might use immigrants to burst or break strikes. The presence of immigrants ensures an 'industrial reserve army' of workers willing and ready to accept menial jobs in the peripheral sector. Out of fear of unemployment, minorities may accept whatever wages employers are willing to offer them. Once again, as a consequence of immigration, minority wage levels remain low.

Other results to comment on (based on analysis not presented) include the fact that immigrants appear to have a marginally significant effect on the industrial sector of minorities. Suggested is that there is some degree of stratification even within the secondary labor market. Immigrants are presumably at the bottom, and directly on top of them are minorities. Immigrants do not appear to influence minority socioeconomic attainment in any significant way, although the negative coefficient suggest that in the long run, minorities may not be helped by increases in immigration of unskilled labor.

Findings from this study indicate that the effects of immigration on the United States labor market are variegated, and they present a perplexing paradox for policy makers. Immigrants affect minorities and whites differently. Historically, immigration appears to have benefitted whites in terms of earnings, socioeconomic attainment, occupational mobility within industry, and employment. When minorities are considered, however, immigration seems to have had opposite effects. Non-whites appear to have lost jobs to immigrants. Their earnings have also been reduced by immigrants. Native minorities and low skilled immigrants seem to be strong competitors and substitutes in the labor market.

Chapter 12

Policy Implications and Recommendations

In both size and composition, the flow of immigrants to the United States has changed remarkably since 1970. As was pointed out in the opening chapters, countries in Latin America and Asia have become important sources of immigration. This change in countries of origin represents a break from previous patterns of immigration to the United States, when new entrants were predominantly from western and northern European countries. As changes in immigrant origins occur, policy makers might at times be guided more by emotions, fear, and in some cases by racial prejudice than by empirical evidence regarding the true nature and effects of the new immigration. Concern about the impact of immigration is especially heightened when researchers whose findings might influence policy makers sometimes allow their own biases to dictate and cloud the outcomes of their research, instead of letting their data do so. Under such circumstances, unfounded, inflammatory, and dangerous conclusions are reached, which if adopted by policy makers can lead to the passage of misguided legislation directed against immigrants. Thus, to make informed policy decisions and to enact fair legislation, it is imperative that policy makers have accurate and objective information about the true consequences of immigration on American society.

This study has shown that in general, continuous immigration is not detrimental to the United States. The evidence shows that immigration has some benefits for the nation. Immigration leads to increases in native earnings, native socioeconomic status, native industrial sector, and considerable decreases in native unemployment. The major implication of this from the point of view of immigration policy is that restrictions on immigration may not in the long run be in the best interest of the United States. Future immigration policy and immigration legislation should aim at greater selectivity of immigrants. Such a process should have U.S. labor market interests (not family reunification) as a priority. This recommendation is based on findings that human capital factors are the most important determinants of various labor market outcomes, including earnings, occupational prestige, socioeconomic attainment, and industrial sectors within which workers are employed in the economy. Thus, immigrant selectivity should be based not on race, sex, or national origin, but on skills that are potential assets for the United States.

For the above to be achieved, a considerable amount of fairness is necessary in current U.S. immigration policies. Past U.S. immigration history has seen amnesty accorded thousands of immigrants that had previously entered the country illegally, or persons that had 'overstayed' their visas illegally. At the same time, it is not uncommon for immigration authorities to harass skilled individuals that have legally entered the United States temporarily, perhaps as students, but later asked to become residents. Ultimately, the impression is given that those who enter the country illegally will be rewarded, but those who enter legally will be punished if they choose to remain. An immigration policy that had labor concerns of the nation in mind would be one that made it easier for skilled individuals to adjust their status based solely upon the labor market needs of the country. Persons with graduate or professional degrees for example, may in the long run be far more valuable to the United States than those entering illegally.

At present, administration of U.S. immigration policies often seems antagonistic towards individuals desiring to remain in the country legally. In fact, without obtaining help through a family member already in the country (through family reunification) , it is now extremely difficult for a person to legally immigrate to the United States, especially if he or she were coming from a third world country. Despite reforms and changes brought about by the Immigration Reform and Control Act of 1986, and amendments through 1996, the tremendous amount of paper work involved in the adjustment of status process, and the hurdles to be crossed seem so insurmountable that skilled individuals desiring to remain in the United States may give up the application process. Some return home, while others fall out of status, overstay visas, and ultimately fall into the dubious class of 'illegal aliens'. At present, the legal options available for changing one's status (from, say a student) to a legal resident are severely limited, and this is partly responsible for the increase in visa over stayers, and hence to the increases in illegal immigration. Frequently finding no other way out to change their status, some that previously entered as nonimmigrants resort to marriage to U.S. citizens. The policy implication is clear. Instead of letting the Immigration and Naturalization Service treat nonimmigrants who ask for change of status as immediate candidates for deportation, the law should make provision for status adjustments in the absence of a prior U.S. family connection. This will help reduce illegal immigration.

Results have shown that in areas with above average concentrations of immigrants, although the overall positive effects of immigration remain, they tend to decrease or disappear. This study offers two policy recommendations based on the above mentioned finding. First, future U.S. immigration policy makers should attempt to spread out new entrants around the country, especially within states that have traditionally had very few numbers of immigrants. One way to begin this is to allocate a place of residence for incoming entrants for a given number of years, say two. The residency requirement can be made a condition for visa issuance. In practice, this recommendation may meet varying degrees of opposition in a free and open society. However, the long-term benefits might outweigh initial public reaction.

A second recommendation is that a new approach be adopted for curbing illegal immigration. States with large immigrant concentrations are likely to be regions with massive illegal immigration. It has been shown that in these areas, immigration may not be beneficial to the United States. Present U.S. immigration policies over emphasize law enforcement and the capture and deportation of illegal immigrants. Consequently, thousands or even millions of dollars are spent every year to combat illegal immigration. However, unless an electrified wall is built along the U.S.-Mexican border (and one along the Canadian border as well) it is highly unlikely that illegal immigration will cease. Then there is increasing evidence that a significant number of 'illegals' or 'potential illegals' enter through the nation's major airports, not through Mexico or Canada. A different approach aimed at reducing illegal immigration should focus on discouraging it from within the sending countries. One suggestion is for the United States to provide economic assistance to Latin American countries from which illegal immigrants come. Perhaps some of the money now being spent on enforcement can be reallocated for this purpose. U.S. corporations may also be encouraged to boost investments in those countries and help create economic opportunities. The chances are high that if good job opportunities exist in their home countries, potential 'illegal immigrants' might find it more attractive to stay home, than come to the United States. Decreases observed in immigration from Europe are linked to a significant extent to the economic recovery on that continent during the past two decades. Illegal immigration from Mexico, Latin American and other developing countries might be reduced if better economic opportunities are created there.

Past analysts have alluded to reduced skill levels among more recent immigrants, and have taken the position that such reductions could have detrimental effects on American society. This study has also found that skill levels of immigrants, especially recent ones, are lower on average than native born citizens. At the same time, analysis has shown that differences in skill levels have not been translated into major earnings disparities between immigrants and natives. Furthermore, immigrant skill levels are not low to a point where they can pose a major threat to the economic health of the United States. A policy action that can possibly improve immigrant skill levels has already been alluded to. Greater selectivity in visa issuance with labor market interests in mind may, in the long run help upset any existing disparities in educational levels among immigrants and natives.

The positive impacts of immigration on the United States seem to depend on the state of the economy. In periods of economic growth, immigrants make significant positive contributions to native earnings and native occupational mobility. During times of economic difficulties, immigration does not appear to benefit the United States. A logical policy recommendation is that immigration quotas be reduced globally when economic recessions are anticipated.

For unexplained reasons, current U.S. immigration policy seems to be based on a rather fallacious premise that immigrants tend to depend on public assistance. Indeed, to be granted a visa, a potential immigrant or even a non-immigrant has to show that he or she will not become a 'public charge' upon arrival in the United States. Results in this book have shown that immigrant reliance on public assistance depends on time. In 1960 and 1970, relative to natives, immigrants had a higher probability of being dependent. This was untrue, however, in 1980. Immigrants were significantly less likely than natives to use public

A good idea to im.

assistance. Past research findings that immigrants tend to rely on U.S. tax payers to support themselves failed to indicate the changing patterns in immigrant public assistance dependence. Strongly suggested in this book is that efforts be made to gather data on immigrants that differentiate refugees from other immigrant groups. It could be that failure to make distinctions between immigrants might have in part led to over generalizations and stereotypes about immigrants' dependence on American tax payers.

It is unreasonable to assume that immigrants might be public charges, given the screening practices of U.S. consular officials abroad. Visa applications routinely request that potential immigrants furnish evidence that they will support themselves while in the United States. In most cases, bank statements and letters of sponsors are required before a visa can be issued.

This study recommends that public policies designed to reduce economic dependence should focus on eliminating unemployment and poverty. Since marital instability appears to be one of the strongest determinants of public assistance reception, such policies should also aim at helping families stay together. Since women and minorities consistently appear to be more dependent (on public assistance), efforts to eliminate prejudice and discrimination in employment should be maintained.

Although immigration was found to be positive for the American population as a whole, there are segments of the society that do not appear to benefit from increases in immigration. Results have shown that non-whites are hurt from increases in immigration. Implied from the findings is that the economy is stratified. Immigrant low-skilled workers tend to be competitors in secondary labor markets with minority workers. While one effect of this is to foster increases in earnings and occupational mobility among whites, there are negative effects which are narrowed on subgroups.

The negative effects of immigration on minorities within the United States cannot be ignored. Continuous immigration of less skilled workers might promote job loss, lower earnings, and reduced occupational mobility for native non-whites. It could create tensions and anger among minorities that could erupt into hostilities, conflicts, riots and violence. Recent racial incidents involving African Americans and Asian and Cuban immigrants in some American cities are ominous warnings of what could happen. In some communities, especially in South Florida and Southern California, there are clearly animosities between Hispanics and African Americans--a form of prejudice not often discussed.

Some analysts and labor leaders have long pointed to competition in the labor market as evidence for adopting restrictive immigration policies. While findings in the present study show evidence of competition, results have shown that low skill levels among minorities constitute a far more important reason for their lower benefits in the economy than immigrants. The real solution to the disadvantaged position of minorities in the U.S. labor market is to address and redress fundamental problems that may be linked to their skill levels. National policies should be adopted that aim at reducing illiteracy, reducing social equality, and increasing skills among non-whites. Strongly suggested from the analysis is that minority status itself in the United States is, and remains a strong deterrent to higher earnings, higher socioeconomic attainment, occupational mobility, and gainful employment. Thus, it seems that the ultimate challenge facing U.S. policy makers and the nation as a whole is to fight prejudice and racial discrimination. Only then can present
disparities between non-whites and the white majority be reduced. Blaming immigrants for the low performance of minorities in the labor market is nothing more than a scapegoating strategy that seeks to sidestep the true causes of minority ills, ills that appear to be strongly rooted in persistent racism and social inequality.

From a policy point of view, restricting immigration solely because immigrants compete with minorities in the secondary labor market for jobs that are obviously low-paying and menial is a tacit admission that such jobs should exist, and that they are for minorities. A sounder and fairer strategy would be one that attempts to provide equal opportunities and incentives to minorities so that they too can move into upper level sectors of the economy.

Appendices

Table A.1

Appendix A

Descriptive Statistics of Variables for Metropolitan Level Analysis, 1980

	Means	Std Dev.	Skewness	Min.	Max.	N
Native Earnings	8359.03	1738.26	1.530	5564.15	14708.72	76
Native SES	30.83	3.32	0.032	23.62	37.90	76
Nat. Industrial Sector	32.35	2.83	0.857	26.85	40.58	76
Pct. Immigrants	8.42	7.02	2.251	0.60	44.60	76
Pct. Aliens	4.12	4.28	2.254	0.00	24.30	76
Native Unemployment	30.81	5.55	-0.209	17.20	42.30	76
Minority Unemployment	5.77	4.32	1.974	0.60	24.90	76
Pct. on Soc. Sec.	5.84	2.03	0.966	2.50	12.20	76
Pct. on Public Assist.	3.53	1.41	0.828	1.50	8.20	76
Pct. College Educated	39.26	8.88	0.281	18.50	61.90	76
Average Education	14.46	0.61	0.112	13.11	15.90	76
Pct. Unskilled Minorit.	2.06	1.78	1.724	0.00	8.70	76
Pct. Non-white	17.52	11.92	2.496	2.60	72.40	76
Pct. Female	52.21	1.41	0.428	49.40	55.50	76
Pct. Unmarried	38.21	5.14	2.030	27.30	66.20	76
Average Weeks Worked	31.84	2.05	0.167	26.49	36.07	76
Pct. Work Disability	9.18	2.27	-0.029	3.90	14.60	76
Pct. Pub. trans. Dis.	1.84	0.67	0.357	0.50	3.70	76
Pct. in Poverty	10.94	3.39	0.338	2.70	23.10	76
Average Age	36.59	1.45	0.233	32.14	40.30	76
Pct. under 25 years	24.96	2.82	0.917	18.20	37.00	76

Table A.2   Effects of Immigration on Native Earnings in Dollars, States with Immigrant Populations 5% or more, 1940 - 1980

Independent Variable	1940	1950	1960	1970	1980
Pct. Immigrants	-19.248[a]	23.425[a]	48.548[b]	48.391[b]	129.460
Std. estimate	-.912	.341	.367	.308	.217
t-ratio	-3.198	3.113	1.865	1.860	1.331
Pct. College Educat.	-7.960	3.579	-.353	30.548[b]	154.566[a]
Std. estimate	-.248	.106	-.004	.303	.706
t-ratio	-1.178	.743	-.017	1.789	5.133
Pct. Female	-10.960[a]	-44.172[a]	-18.802	194.062[b]	-15.109
Std. estimate	-.798	-.559	-.116	.447	-.018
t-ratio	-2.823	-5.333	-.458	2.495	-.107
Average Age	5.817	60.949[c]	128.472	-52.740	-755.780[b]
Std. estimate	.100	.218	.262	-.085	-.338
t-ratio	.433	1.580	1.220	-.464	-1.829
Ave. Weeks Worked	2.231	465.095[a]	-.829	111.042[b]	4.940
Std. estimate	.009	.541	-.003	.370	.006
t-ratio	.046	5.076	-.014	2.048	.042
R^2	.560	.815	.188	.381	.729
Adj. R^2	.391	.763	.003	.247	.658
Number of Observations	19	24	28	29	25

a significant at $p < .01$. (one-tailed test).
b significant at $p < .05$. (one-tailed test).
c significant at $p < .10$. (one-tailed test).

Table A.3   Effects of Immigration on Native Earnings, 1980, MSAs with 10% or more of Immigrants

Independent Variable	Earnings in Dollars	Log of Earnings
Percent Immigrants		
Std. estimate	10.534	.002
t-values	.041	.074
	.478	.948
Average Weeks Worked		
Std. estimate	-121.464	-.002
t-values	-.150	-.018
	-.656	-.087
Average Age		
Std. estimate	586.252[a]	.047[a]
t-values	.363	.287
	3.226	2.794
Percent College Educated		
Std. estimate	87.789[a]	.008[a]
t-values	.376	.342
	3.332	3.319
Percent Females		
Std. estimate	-473.402[a]	-.043[a]
t-values	-.262	-.235
	-2.611	-2.562
Percent with Work Disability		
Std. estimate	-494.435[b]	-.048[a]
t-values	-.578	-.546
	-2.181	-2.256
R^2	.881	.901
Adj. R^2	.841	.868
Number of Observations	25	25

a Significant at $p < .01$ (one-tailed test).
b Significant at $p < .05$ (one-tailed test).
c Significant at $p < .10$ (one-tailed test).

Table A.4   Effects of Immigration on Native Prestige and SES, 1960 - 1980, States with 5% or More Immigrants

Independent Variable	Native Prestige		Native SES
	1960	1970	1980
Percent Immigrants			
Std. estimate	.029	.397[a]	-.014
t-ratio	.045	.462	-.018
	.253	3.242	-.105
Percent Female			
Std. estimate	.223	.160	.280
t-ratio	.280	.067	.256
	1.134	.468	1.149
Percent Non-white			
Std. estimate	.063c	.045	-.044
t-ratio	.289	.127	-.231
	1.390	.868	-1.302
Average Education			
Std. estimate	3.795[a]	2.725[a]	4.756[a]
t-ratio	.534	.398	.914
	2.575	2.746	5.139
Average Weeks Worked			
Std. estimate	.115	.674[a]	.008
t-ratio	.090	.411	.007
	.485	2.843	.046
R²	.329	.557	.639
Adj. R²	.177	.461	.543
Number of Observations	28	29	25

a significant at p < .01. (one-tailed test).
b significant at p < .05. (one-tailed test).
c significant at p < .10. (one-tailed test).

Table A.5   Metropolitan Level Analysis of the Effects of Immigration On Native Socioeconomic Status, 1980: MSAs with Immigrants 10% or More of Population

Independent Variable	b	Beta	t-ratio	Prob.
Percent Immigrants	.081	.178	3.455	.000
Average Weeks Worked	.670	.470	7.041	.000
Percent Non-white	-.019	-.073	-1.388	.091
Percent Females	.000	.000	.004	.498
Average Educational Attainment	3.006	.585	9.415	.000
R^2		.957		
Adj. R^2		.946		
Number of Observations		25		

Table A.6   Effects of Immigration on Native Industrial Sector, States with Immigrant Populations 5% or more, 1960 - 1980

Independent Variable	1960	1970	1980
Percentage Immigrants			
Std. estimate	.148[b]	.380[a]	-.092
	.151	.492	-.111
t-ratio	1.721	3.328	-.555
Percentage Female			
Std. estimate	-.151	.754[b]	.756[b]
	-.126	.353	.666
t-ratio	-.430	2.375	2.495
Percentage Non-white			
Std. estimate	-.040	-.033	-.128[a]
	-.121	-.104	-.641
t-ratio	-.493	-.686	-3.007
Average Education			
Std. estimate	-1.378	2.258[b]	3.987[a]
	-.035	.366	.736
t-ratio	-.144	2.443	3.460
Average Weeks Worked			
Std. estimate	-.116	.548[b]	.309
	-.060	.371	.267
t-ratio	-.274	2.481	1.398
R^2	.103	.525	.483
Adj. R^2	.003	.422	.346
Number of Observations	28	29	25

a significant at $p < .01$.
b significant at $p < .05$.
c significant at $p < .10$.

Table A.7   Metropolitan Level Analysis of the Effects of Immigration on Native Industrial Sector, 1980: MSAs with Immigrant Populations 10% or more

Independent Variable	b	Beta	t-ratio	Prob.
Percent Immigrants	-.014	-.029	-.220	.414
Average Weeks Worked	1.373	.920	2.729	.007
Percent Non-white	-.027	-.098	.702	.246
Percent Females	-.886	-.266	-1.854	.040
Average Educational Attainment	-.430	-.080	-.423	.339
Percent with Work Disability	.360	.228	.609	.275
R^2		.739		
Adj. R^2		.651		
Number of Observations		25		

Table A.8   Determinants of Unemployment, 1980

Independent Variable	b	Beta	t-ratio	Prob.
Immigrant Status	.020	.014	4.722	.000
Race	.023	.020	12.249	.000
Age	-.001	-.031	-17.213	.000
Region	.007	.007	4.660	.000
Children under 18	.018	.056	32.628	.000
Marital status	.040	.041	22.959	.000
Education	-.022	-.150	-88.663	.000
Sex	.224	.238	151.514	.000
Work Disability	.319	.194	109.417	.000
Public Transp. Disability	.158	.047	27.026	.000
Years Since Immigration	-.002	-.021	-8.603	.000
English Proficiency	.004	.007	2.944	.003
R^2		.145		
Number of Observations		347,665		

Table A.9 Metropolitan Level Results of the Effects of Immigration on Unemployment: MSAs with Immigrants 10% or more of the Population, 1980.

Independent Variables	Native Unemployment	Minority Unemployment
Percentage Immigrants		
Std. estimate	-.309[a]	-.045
	-.427	-.117
t-statistic	-6.482	-.646
Percentage with less than High School Education		
Std. estimate	-.161[a]	---
	-.245	---
t-statistic	-2.255	---
Percentage Non-white		
Std. estimate	.089[a]	---
	.212	---
t-statistic	3.072	---
Percentage Female		
Std. estimate	-.307	.090
	-.060	.033
t-statistic	-.846	.199
Average Age		
Std. estimate	1.242[a]	---
	.273	---
t-statistic	3.162	---
Percentage with Work Disability		
Std. estimate	3.320[a]	.025
	.963	.019
t-statistic	10.514	.097
Percentage Divorced		
Std. estimate	-.266[a]	.193[c]
	-.195	.267
t-statistic	-2.591	1.387

Table A.9 Continued

Percentage Minorities without Skills		
Std. estimate	—	2.350[a]
t-statistic	—	.753
	—	4.293
Percentage under 25 years		
Std. estimate	—	.201
t-statistic	—	.164
	—	.890
R^2	.952	.615
Adj. R^2	.932	.486
Number of Observations	25	25

a significant at p < .01 (one-tailed test)
b significant at p < .05 (one-tailed test)
c significant at p < .10 (one-tailed test)

Table A.10

Determinants of Public Assistance Reception, 1980

Independent Variable	b	Beta	t-ratio	Prob.
Immigrant Status	-.016	-.028	-7.558	.000
Alien Status	-.014	-.020	-7.599	.000
Years Since Immigration	.000	.013	4.783	.000
Race	.035	.075	44.205	.000
Poverty	.069	.116	66.851	.000
Unemployment	.015	.038	15.408	.000
Age	.000	.024	13.138	.000
Region	.007	.019	11.712	.000
Children under 18	-.000	-.005	-2.747	.006
Marital Status	.033	.087	46.906	.000
Education	-.003	-.060	-34.060	.000
English Proficiency	-.000	-.003	-1.282	.199
Sex	.017	.045	26.858	.000
Work Disability	.082	.125	67.474	.000
Public Trans. Disability	.076	.056	31.557	.000
Weeks Worked	-.000	-.060	-23.247	.000
R^2		.104		
Number of Observations		347,665		

Table A.11

Determinants of Social Security Reception, 1980

Independent Variable	b	Beta	t-ratio	Prob.
Immigrant Status	-.002	-.002	-.693	.489
Alien Status	-.016	-.018	-7.197	.000
Years Since Immigration	.000	.005	2.145	.032
Work Disability	.118	.149	83.341	.000
Public Trans. Disability	.095	.058	34.033	.000
Race	-.005	-.009	-5.306	.000
Sex	-.021	-.046	-28.520	.000
Age	.004	.228	129.084	.000
Marital Status	.046	.101	56.383	.000
Poverty	-.026	-.037	-21.899	.000
Unemployment	.030	.063	26.366	.000
Education	-.003	-.037	-21.484	.000
Weeks Worked	-.002	-.165	-66.412	.000
English Proficiency	.007	.022	9.953	.000
Region	-.003	-.006	-3.754	.000
R^2		.167		
Number of Observations		347,665		

Appendix B

Table B.1   Effects of Immigration on Native Earnings in Dollars, States with Immigrant Populations 5% or more, 1940 - 1980

Independent Variable	1940	1950	1960	1970	1980
Pct. Immigrants					
Std. estimate	-19.248[a]	23.425[a]	48.548[b]	48.391[b]	129.460
t-ratio	-.912	.341	.367	.308	.217
	-3.198	3.113	1.865	1.860	1.331
Pct. College Educat.					
Std. estimate	-7.960	3.579	-.353	30.548[b]	154.566[a]
t-ratio	-.248	.106	-.004	.303	.706
	-1.178	.743	-.017	1.789	5.133
Pct. Female					
Std. estimate	-10.960[a]	-44.172[a]	-18.802	194.062[b]	-15.109
t-ratio	-.798	-.559	-.116	.447	-.018
	-2.823	-5.333	-.458	2.495	-.107
Average Age					
Std. estimate	5.817	60.949[c]	128.472	-52.740	-755.780[b]
t-ratio	.100	.218	.262	-.085	-.338
	.433	1.580	1.220	-.464	-1.829
Ave. Weeks Worked					
Std. estimate	2.231	465.095[a]	-.829	111.042[b]	4.940
t-ratio	.009	.541	-.003	.370	.006
	.046	5.076	-.014	2.048	.042
R^2	.560	.815	.188	.381	.729
Adj. R^2	.391	.763	.003	.247	.658
Number of Observations	19	24	28	29	25

a   significant at $p < .01$. (one-tailed test).
b   significant at $p < .05$. (one-tailed test).
c   significant at $p < .10$. (one-tailed test).

Appendix C

Table C.1		
	Effects of Immigration on Native Earnings, 1980, MSAs with 10% or more of Immigrants	
Independent Variable	Earnings in Dollars	Log of Earnings
Percent Immigrants		
Std. estimate	10.534	.002
t-value	.041	.074
	.478	.948
Average Weeks Worked		
Std. estimate	-121.464	-.002
t-value	-.150	-.018
	-.656	-.087
Average Age		
Std. estimate	586.252[a]	.047[a]
t-value	.363	.287
	3.226	2.794
Percent College Educated		
Std. estimate	87.789[a]	.008[a]
t-value	.376	.342
	3.332	3.319
Percent Females		
Std. estimate	-473.402[a]	-.043[a]
t-value	-.262	-.235
	-2.611	-2.562
Percent with Work Disability		
Std. estimate	-494.435[b]	-.048[a]
t-value	-.578	-.546
	-2.181	-2.256
R^2	.881	.901
Adj. R^2	.841	.868
Number of Observations	25	25

a Significant at $p < .01$ (one-tailed test).
b Significant at $p < .05$ (one-tailed test).
c Significant at $p < .10$ (one-tailed test).

Appendix D

Table D.1   Effects of Immigration on Native Prestige and SES, 1960 - 1980, States with 5% or More Immigrants

Independent Variable	Native Prestige		Native SES
	1960	1970	1980
Percent Immigrants			
Std. estimate	.029	.397[a]	-.014
t-ratio	.045	.462	-.018
	.253	3.242	-.105
Percent Female			
Std. estimate	.223	.160	.280
t-ratio	.280	.067	.256
	1.134	.468	1.149
Percent Non-white			
Std. estimate	.063[c]	.045	-.044
t-ratio	.289	.127	-.231
	1.390	.868	-1.302
Average Education			
Std. estimate	3.795[a]	2.725[a]	4.756[a]
t-ratio	.534	.398	.914
	2.575	2.746	5.139
Average Weeks Worked			
Std. estimate	.115	.674[a]	.008
t-ratio	.090	.411	.007
	.485	2.843	.046
R^2	.329	.557	.639
Adj. R^2	.177	.461	.543
Number of Observations	28	29	25

a   significant at p < .01. (one-tailed test).
b   significant at p < .05. (one-tailed test).
c   significant at p < .10. (one-tailed test).

Appendix E

Table E.1   Metropolitan Level Analysis of the Effects of Immigration on Native Socioeconomic Status, 1980: MSAs with Immigrants 10% or More of Population

Independent Variable	b	Beta	t-value	Prob.
Percent Immigrants	.081	.178	3.455	.000
Average Weeks Worked	.670	.470	7.041	.000
Percent Non-white	-.019	-.073	-1.388	.091
Percent Females	.000	.000	.004	.498
Average Educational Attainment	3.006	.585	9.415	.000
R^2		.957		
Adj. R^2		.946		
Number of Observations		25		

Appendix F

Table F.1 Effects of Immigration on Native Industrial Sector, States with Immigrant Populations 5% or more, 1960 - 1980

Independent Variable	1960	1970	1980
Percentage Immigrants			
Std. estimate	.148[b]	.380[a]	-.092
	.151	.492	-.111
t-ratio	1.721	3.328	-.555
Percentage Female			
Std. estimate	-.151	.754[b]	.756[b]
	-.126	.353	.666
t-ratio	-.430	2.375	2.495
Percentage Non-white			
Std. estimate	-.040	-.033	-.128[a]
	-.121	-.104	-.641
t-ratio	-.493	-.686	-3.007
Average Education			
Std. estimate	-1.378	2.258[b]	3.987[a]
	-.035	.366	.736
t-ratio	-.144	2.443	3.460
Average Weeks Worked			
Std. estimate	-.116	.548[b]	.309
	-.060	.371	.267
t-ratio	-.274	2.481	1.398
R^2	.103	.525	.483
Adj. R^2	.003	.422	.346
Number of Observations	28	29	25

a significant at $p < .01$.
b significant at $p < .05$.
c significant at $p < .10$.

Appendix G

Table G.1   Metropolitan Level Analysis of the Effects of Immigration on Native Industrial Sector, 1980: MSAs with Immigrant Populations 10% or more

Independent Variable	b	Beta	t-value	Prob.
Percent Immigrants	-.014	-.029	-.220	.414
Average Weeks Worked	1.373	.920	2.729	.007
Percent Non-white	-.027	-.098	.702	.246
Percent Females	-.886	-.266	-1.854	.040
Average Educational Attainment	-.430	-.080	-.423	.339
Percent with Work Disability	.360	.228	.609	.275
R^2		.739		
Adj. R^2		.651		
Number of Observations		25		

Appendix H

Table H.1

Determinants of Unemployment, 1980

Independent Variable	b	Beta	t-ratio	Prob.
Immigrant Status	.020	.014	4.722	.000
Race	.023	.020	12.249	.000
Age	-.001	-.031	-17.213	.000
Region	.007	.007	4.660	.000
Children under 18	.018	.056	32.628	.000
Marital status	.040	.041	22.959	.000
Education	-.022	-.150	-88.663	.000
Sex	.224	.238	151.514	.000
Work Disability	.319	.194	109.417	.000
Public Transp. Disability	.158	.047	27.026	.000
Years Since Immigration	-.002	-.021	-8.603	.000
English Proficiency	.004	.007	2.944	.003
R^2		.145		
Number of Observations		347,665		

Appendix I

Table I.1 Metropolitan Level Results of the Effects of Immigration on Unemployment: MSAs with Immigrants 10% or more of the Population, 1980.

Independent Native Variables	Minority Unemployment	Unemployment
Percentage Immigrants		
Std. estimate	-.309[a]	-.045
	-.427	-.117
t-statistic	-6.482	-.646
Percentage with less than High School Education		
Std. estimate	-.161[a]	---
	-.245	---
t-statistic	-2.255	---
Percentage Non-white		
Std. estimate	.089[a]	---
	.212	---
t-statistic	3.072	---
Percentage Female		
Std. estimate	-.307	.090
	-.060	.033
t-statistic	-.846	.199
Average Age		
Std. estimate	1.242[a]	---
	.273	---
t-statistic	3.162	---
Percentage with Work Disability		
Std. estimate	3.320[a]	.025
	.963	.019
t-statistic	10.514	.097

Table I.1   Continued

Percentage Divorced		
Std. estimate	-.266[a]	.193[c]
t-statistic	-.195	.267
	-2.591	1.387
Percentage Minorities without Skills		
Std. estimate	---	2.350[a]
t-statistic	---	.753
	---	4.293
Percentage under 25 years		
Std. estimate	---	.201
t-statistic	---	.164
	---	.890
R^2	.952	.615
Adj. R^2	.932	.486
Number of Observations	25	25

a significant at $p < .01$ (one-tailed test)
b significant at $p < .05$ (one-tailed test)
c significant at $p < .10$ (one-tailed test)

Appendix J

Table J.1

Determinants of Public Assistance Reception, 1980

Independent Variable	b	Beta	t-ratio	Prob.
Immigrant Status	-.016	-.028	-7.558	.000
Alien Status	-.014	-.020	-7.599	.000
Years Since Immigration	.000	.013	4.783	.000
Race	.035	.075	44.205	.000
Poverty	.069	.116	66.851	.000
Unemployment	.015	.038	15.408	.000
Age	.000	.024	13.138	.000
Region	.007	.019	11.712	.000
Children under 18	-.000	-.005	-2.747	.006
Marital Status	.033	.087	46.906	.000
Education	-.003	-.060	-34.060	.000
English Proficiency	-.000	-.003	-1.282	.199
Sex	.017	.045	26.858	.000
Work Disability	.082	.125	67.474	.000
Public Trans. Disability	.076	.056	31.557	.000
Weeks Worked	-.000	-.060	-23.247	.000
R^2		.104		
Number of Observations		347,665		

Appendix K

Table K.1   Determinants of Social Security Reception, 1980

Independent Variable	b	Beta	t-ratio	Prob.
Immigrant Status	-.002	-.002	-.693	.489
Alien Status	-.016	-.018	-7.197	.000
Years Since Immigration	.000	.005	2.145	.032
Work Disability	.118	.149	83.341	.000
Public Trans. Disability	.095	.058	34.033	.000
Race	-.005	-.009	-5.306	.000
Sex	-.021	-.046	-28.520	.000
Age	.004	.228	129.084	.000
Marital Status	.046	.101	56.383	.000
Poverty	-.026	-.037	-21.899	.000
Unemployment	.030	.063	26.366	.000
Education	-.003	-.037	-21.484	.000
Weeks Worked	-.002	-.165	-66.412	.000
English Proficiency	.007	.022	9.953	.000
Region	-.003	-.006	-3.754	.000
R^2		.167		
Number of Observations		347,665		

References

References

Abott, Edith. 1926. *Historical Aspects of the Immigration Problem.* Chicago: University of Chicago Press.

Abrams, E. and F. Abrams. 1975. "Immigration Policy--Who Gets in and Why?" *The Public Interest* 38:3-29.

Averitt, Robert. 1968. *The Dual Economy.* New York: W. W. Norton.

Bach, R. L. and M. Tienda. 1984. "Contemporary Immigration and Refugee Movements and Employment." Pp. 37-82 in *Immigration Issues and Policies,* edited by V. M. Briggs and M. Tienda. Salt Lake City, UT: Olympus Publishing Company.

Bailey, Thomas R. 1987. *Immigrant and Native Workers: Contrasts and Competition.* Boulder: Westview Press.

Bean, Frank D. and T. A. Sullivan. 1985. "Confronting the Problem." *Society* 22(4):67-72.

Bean, Frank D., Edward E. Telles, and B. Lindsay Lowell. 1987. "Undocumented Migration to the United States: Perceptions and Evidence." *Population and Development Review* 13(4):671-690.

Bean, Frank D., B. Lindsay Lowell, and Lowell J. Taylor. 1988. "Undocumented Mexican Immigrants and the Earnings of Other Workers in the United States." *Demography* 25(1):35-52.

Bean, Frank D., George Vernez, and Charles B. Keely. 1989. *Opening and Closing the Doors: Evaluating Immigration Reform and Control.* Santa Monica and Washington, DC: The Rand Corporation and The Urban Institute.

Beck, E. M., P. M. Horan, and C. M. Tolbert II. 1978. "Stratification in a Dual Economy: A Sectoral Model of Earnings Determination." *American Sociological Review* 43:704-720.

Becker, Gary S. 1975. *Human Capital.* New York: Columbia University Press.

Bernard, W. S. 1953. "Economic Effects of Immigration." Pp. 50-70 in *Immigration: An American Dilemma,* edited by B.M. Ziegler. Boston: D.C. Heath and Company.

Bernard, W. S. 1965. "America's Immigration Policy: Its Evolution and Sociology." *International Migration* 2(4):235.

Berry, William, D. and Stanley Feldman. 1985. *Multiple Regression in Practice*. Beverly Hills, CA: Sage Publications.

Bibb, R. and W. H. Form. 1977. "The Effects of Industrial, Occupational, and Sex Stratification in Blue-Collar Markets." *Social Forces* 55:974-996.

Blau, Francine D. 1984. "The Use of Transfer Payments by Immigrants." *Industrial and Labor Relations Review* 37(2):222-239.

Blueston, B., W. M. Murphy, and M. Stevenson. 1973. *Low Wages and the Working Poor*. Ann Arbor, MI: Institute of Labor and Industrial Relations, University of Michigan and Wayne State University.

Bonacich, E. 1972. "A Theory of Ethnic Antagonism: The Split Labor Market." *American Sociological Review* 37:547-549.

Bonacich, E. 1976. "Advanced Capitalism and Black/White Relations: A Split Labor Market Interpretation." *American Sociological Review* 41:34-51.

Borjas, G. J. 1983. "The Substitutability of Black, Hispanic and White Labor." *Economic Inquiry* 21:93-106.

Borjas, G. J. 1984. "The Impact of Immigrants on the Earnings of the Native-Born." Pp. 83-126 in *Immigration: Issues and Policies*, edited by V.M. Briggs and M. Tienda. Salt Lake City, UT: Olympus Publishing Company.

Borjas, G. J. 1986. "The Sensitivity of Labor Demand Functions to Choice of Dependent Variable." *Review of Economics and Statistics* 68:58-66.

Borjas, G. J. 1987. "Immigrants, Minorities, and Labor Market Competition." *Industrial and Labor Relations Review* 40(3):382-392.

Borjas, G. J. and M. Tienda. 1987. "The Economic Consequences of Immigration." *Science* 235:645-651.

Borjas, George J. and Stephen J. Trejo. 1991. "Immigrant Participation in the Welfare System." *Industrial and Labor Relations Review* 44:195-211.

Borjas, George J. 1994. "The Economics of Immigration." *Journal of Economic Literature* 32:1667-1717.

214

Bouvier, Leon F. 1981. *The Impact of Immigration on the Size of the U.S. Population*. Washington, DC: Population Reference Bureau.

Bouvier, Leon F. 1983. "U.S. Immigration: Effects on Population Growth and Structure". Pp. 193-209 in *U.S. Immigration and Refugee Policy*, edited by Mary M. Kritz. Lexington, MA: D.C. Heath and Company.

Briggs, Vernon M. 1975a. Illegal Aliens: The Need for a More Restrictive Border Policy." *Social Science Quarterly* 56:477-484.

Briggs, Vernon M. 1975b. "Mexican Workers in the United States Labor Market: A Contemporary Dilemma." *International Labour Review* 112(5):351-368.

Briggs, Vernon M. 1984a. *Immigration Policy and the American Labor Force*. Baltimore, MD: Johns Hopkins University Press.

Briggs, Vernon M. 1984b. "Employment Trends and Contemporary Immigration Policy: The Macro Implication." Pp. 1-34 in *Immigration: Issues and Policies*, edited by V. M. Briggs and M. Tienda. Salt Lake City, UT: Olympus Publishing Company.

Briggs, Vernon, M. 1987. "The Growth and Composition of the U.S. Labor Force." *Science* 238:176-180.

Browning, H. and J. Singlemann. 1978. "The Transformation of the U.S. Labor Force: The Interaction of Industry and Occupation." *Politics and Society* 3-4:481-509.

Cafferty, P. S. J., B. R. Chiswick, A. M. Greeley, and T. A. Sullivan. 1983. *The Dilemma of American Immigration: Beyond the Golden Door*. New Brunswick, NJ: Transaction Books.

Cain, G. G. 1975. *The Challenge of Dual and Radical Theories of the Labor Market to Orthodox Theory*. Discussion Paper, Institute for Research on Poverty, University of Wisconsin, Madison.

Carlson, A. W. 1985. "One Century of Foreign Immigration to the United States: 1880 to 1979." *International Migration* 23(3):309-334.

Chang, Chin-Fen. 1989. Resource or Vulnerabilities? *The Structural Determinants of Economic Returns in American Manufacturing, 1950-1980*. Ph.D. Dissertation, Department of Sociology, The Ohio State University, Columbus, Ohio.

Chen, T. J. 1987. "The Welfare Effects of Illegal Immigration." *Journal of International Economics* 23(3-4):315-328.

Chiswick, Barry R. 1978. "The Effect of Americanization on the Earnings of Foreign-born Men." *Journal of Political Economy* 86(5):897-927.

Chiswick, Barry R. 1984. "Illegal Aliens in the United States Labor Market: Analysis of Occupational Attainment and Earnings." *International Migration Review* 18(3):715-732.

Chiswick, Barry R. 1986. "Is the New Immigration Less Skilled than the Old?" *Journal of Labor Economics* 4(2):168-192.

Cornelius, Wayne A. 1978. *Mexican Migration to the United States: Causes, Consequences and U.S. Response.* M.I.T.: Center for International Studies.

Cornelius, Wayne A. 1980. "Mexican Immigration: Causes and Consequences for Mexico." Pp. 68-84 in *Sourcebook on the New Immigration: Implications for the United States and the International Community*, edited by Roy Simon Bryce-LaPorte. New Brunswick, NJ: Transaction Books.

Davis, Kingsley, and Wilbert E. Moore. 1945. "Some Principles of Stratification." *American Sociological Review* 10:242-247.

Defrauds, Gregory, and A. Marshall. 1984. "Immigration and Wage Growth in U.S. Manufacturing in the 1970s." Pp. 148-156 in *Proceedings of the Thirty-Sixth Annual Meeting Dec. 28-30, 1983 San Francisco*, edited by Barbara D. Dennis, Industrial Research Association.

Diewert, W. E. 1971. "An Application of the Shephard Duality Theorem: A Generalized Leontief Production Function." *Journal of Political Economy* 70:481-507.

Doeringer, P. and M. Piore. 1971. *International Labor Markets and Manpower Analysis.* Lexington: D.C. Heath.

Duncan, Gregg J. 1984. *Years of Poverty Years of Plenty.* Ann Arbor, MI: Institute for Social Research, University of Michigan.

Edwards, R. C. 1975a. *Labor Market Segmentation.* Lexington: D.C. Heath.

Edwards, R. C. 1975b. "The Social Relations of Production in the Firm and Labor Market Structure." In *Labor Market Segmentation*, edited by R. C. Edwards et al. Lexington: D.C. Heath.

216

Fallows, James. 1985. "Immigration: How It's Affecting Us." Pp. 8-13 in *The Problem of Immigration*, edited by Steven Anzovin. New York: The H. W. Wilson Company.

Fauriol, Georges. 1985. "U.S. Immigration Policy and the National Interest." Pp. 96-116 in *The Problem of Immigration*, edited by Steven Anzovin. New York: The H. W. Wilson Company.

Freeman, R. B. 1988. *NBER Summary Report: Immigration, Trade, and the Labor Market*. Cambridge, MA: National Bureau of Economic Research.

Fuchs, Lawrence H. 1984. "Cultural Pluralism and the Future of American Unity: The Impact of Illegal Aliens." *International Migration Review* 18(3):800-813.

General Accounting Office. 1986. Illegal Aliens: *Limited Research Suggests Illegal Aliens May Displace Native Workers*. Washington, DC: Government Printing Office.

Gerdes, C. 1977. "The Fundamental Contradiction in the Neo-Classical Theory of Income Distribution." *Review of Radical Political Economics* 9:39-64.

Glenn, Norval D. 1977. *Cohort Analysis*. Sage University Paper Series on Quantitative Applications in the Social Sciences, Series no. 07-005. Beverly Hills and London: Sage Publications.

Gordon, M. 1972. *Theories of Poverty and Underemployment*. Lexington: Lexington Books.

Greenwood, Michael J. 1983. "Regional Economic Aspects of Immigrant Location Patterns in the United States." Pp. 237-247 in *U.S. Immigration and Refugee Policy*, edited by Mary M. Kritz. Lexington, MA: D.C. Heath and Company.

Grossman, Jean B. 1982. "The Substitutability of Natives and Immigrants in Production." *Review of Economics and Statistics* 54(4):596-603.

Harper, Elizabeth J. 1975. *Immigration Laws of the United States*. Indianapolis, IN: Bobbs-Merrill.

Harris, J. R. and M. Todaro. 1970. "Migration, Unemployment and Development: A Two Sector Analysis." *American Economic Review* 60:139-149.

Hauser, Robert M. 1980. "On Stratification in a Dual Economy." *American Sociological Review* 45(5):702-712.

Hoffman, Abraham. 1978. "Mexican Repatriation During the Great Depression." In *Immigrants and Immigrants: Perspectives on Mexican Labor Migration to the United States*, edited by Arthur F. Corwin. Westport, CT: Greenwood Press.

Hodson, Randy, and Robert Kaufman. 1982. "Economic Dualism: A Critical Review." *American Sociological Review* 47:727-739.

Hutchinson, Edward P. 1981. *Legislative History of American Immigration Policy, 1798-1965*. Philadelphia: University of Pennsylvania Press.

Hutchinson, Edward P. 1956. *Immigrants and their Children, 1850-1950*. New York: John Wiley.

ICPSR Inter-University Consortium for Political and Social Research. 1987. *United States Microdata Samples Extract File, 1940-1980: Demographics of Aging*. Ann Arbor, MI: Inter-University Consortium for Political and Social Research.

Jaffe, Abram J., Ruth M. Cullen, and Thomas D. Boswell. 1980. *The Changing Demography of Spanish Americans*. New York: Academic Press.

Johnson, George E. 1980. "The Labor Market Effects of Immigration." *Industrial and Labor Relations Review* 33(3):331-341.

Jones, F. E. 1987. Age at Immigration and Education." *International Migration Review*.

Jones, Harry. 1926. *Migration and Business Cycles*. New York: The Macmillan Company.

Kerr, Clark. 1954. "The Balkanization of Labor Markets." In *Labor Mobility and Economic Opportunity*, edited by E. W. Bakke. Cambridge, MA: MIT Press.

King, Allan G., Lindsay Lowell, and Frank D. Bean. 1986. "The Effects of Hispanic Immigrants on the Earnings of Native Americans." *Social Science Quarterly* 67(4):673-689.

Kposowa, Augustine J. 1986. *The Relationship Between Opportunities and Interregional Migration in Sierra Leone*. M.A. Thesis, University of Cincinnati, Cincinnati, Ohio.

Kposowa, Augustine J. 1987a. "The Effects of Opportunities and Cultural Differences on Interregional Migration in Sierra Leone." *African Urban Quarterly* 4(2):378-396.

218

Kposowa, Augustine J. 1987b. "On the Interpretation of Logistic Regression: Determinants of Marijuana Legalization." Unpublished Manuscript, Department of Sociology, The Ohio State University, Columbus, Ohio.

Kposowa, Augustine J. 1995. "Immigration and Public Dependence in the U.S.: Approaches to Presenting Logistic Regression Results." *Applied Behavioral Science Review* 3:65-83.

Lamm, Richard, and Imhoff, Gary. 1985. *The Immigration Time Bomb*. New York: Truman Talley Books.

Lebergott, Stanley. 1964. *Manpower in Economic Growth*. New York: McGraw-Hill.

Li, Wen L. 1976. "Chinese Americans: Exclusion from the Melting Pot." Pp. 297-324 in *The Minority Report*, edited by A. G. Dworkin and R. J. Dworkin. New York: Praeger.

Li, Wen L. 1981. "Immigration and the Dual Labor Market." *Proceedings of the American Statistical Association*, Social Sciences Section.

Lord, George F. III, and William W. Falk. 1980. "An Exploratory Analysis of Individualistic Versus Structuralist Explanations of Income." *Social Forces* 59(2):376-391.

Lutton, Wayne and John Tanton. 1994. *The Immigration Invasion*. Petoskey, MI.: Social Contract Press.

Maram, Sheldon L. 1980. *Hispanic Workers in the Garment and Restaurant Industries in Los Angeles County*. Monograph in U.S.-Mexican Studies, No. 12, San Diego.

Marshall, Ray. 1984. "Immigration: An International Economic Perspective." *International Migration Review* 18(3):593-612.

Marshall, Ray. 1987. "Controlling Illegal Immigration." *Hearings Before the Joint Economic Committee on Economic and Demographic Consequences of Immigration*. Washington, DC: Government Printing Office.

Massey, Douglas S. 1981. "Dimensions of the New Immigration to the United States and the Prospects for Assimilation." *Annual Review of Sociology* 7:57-85.

Massey, Douglas S. 1987. "Do Undocumented Migrants Earn Lower Wages?" *International Migration Review* 21:236-274.

Matta, Benjamin N. and Popp, Anthony V. 1988. "Immigration and the Earnings of Youth in the U.S." *International Migration Review* 22(1):104-116.

McCarthy, Kevin F. and R. Burciaga Valdez. 1986. *Current and Future Effects of Mexican Immigration in California.* Santa Monica: The Rand Corporation.

McManus, W. S. 1987. "Essay on Legal and Illegal Immigration." *Journal of Regional Science* 27(3):439-491.

Miller, Michael V. 1981. *Economic Growth and Change Along the U.S.-Mexican Border: The Case of Brownsville, Texas.* Working Paper, University of Texas at San Antonio. Human Management Resources Program.

Mincer, J. 1970. "The Distribution of Labor Incomes: A Survey with Special Reference to the Human Capital Approach." *Journal of Economic Literature* 8:1-26.

Mincer, J. 1974. *Schooling, Experience, and Earnings.* New York: National Bureau of Economic Research.

Mines, Richard, and Ricardo Anzaldual. 1982. *New Migrants vs Old Migrants: Alternative Labor Market Structures in the California Citrus Industry.* Monograph in U.S.-Mexican Studies, San Diego.

Morgan, S. P., and J. D. Teachman. 1988. "Logistic Regression: Description, Examples, and Comparisons." *Journal of Marriage and the Family* 50:929-936.

Muller, Thomas, and Thomas J. Espenshade. 1985. *The Fourth Immigrant Wave: California's Newest Immigrants.* Washington, DC: The Urban Institute Press.

Murphy, Dwight D. 1994. "The World Population Explosion and the Cost of Uncontrolled Immigration." *Journal of Social, Political and Economic Studies* 19:481-511.

Muth, R. E. 1971. "Migration: Chicken or Egg?" *Southern Economic Journal* 37(3)295-306.

Nagi, Saad Z. 1989. "Health Variables and Labor Force Attachment." Unpublished Manuscript, Department of Sociology, The Ohio State University, Columbus, Ohio.

Nelli, Humbert S. 1983. *From Immigrants to Ethnics: The Italian Americans.* New York: Oxford University Press.

220

NORC. 1980. *General Social Surveys, 1972-1980: Cumulative Codebook*. Chicago: National Opinion Research Center.

North, David S. and William G. Weisberg. 1974. *Immigrants and the Labor Market*. Washington, DC: Government Printing Office.

North, David S. and Marion F. Houston. 1976. *The Characteristics and Role of Illegal Aliens in the U.S. Labor Market: An Exploratory Study*. Washington, DC: Linton and Company.

North, David S. and A. LeBel. 1978. *Manpower and Immigration Policies in the United States*. Report to the National Commission for Manpower Policy.

O'Connor, James. 1973. *The Fiscal Crisis of the State*. New York: St. Martin Press.

Petersen, Trond. 1985. "A Comment on Presenting Results From Logit and Probit Models." *American Sociological Review* 50:130-131.

Pinkney, Alphoneso. 1993. *Black Americans*. Englewood Cliffs: Prentice-Hall.

Piore, M. J. 1972. *Notes for a Theory of Labor Stratification*. Paper No. 41, Center for Educational Policy Research, Graduate School of Education, Harvard University, Cambridge, MA.

Piore, M. J. 1975. "Notes for a Theory of Labor Market Segmentation." Pp. 125-150 in *Labor Market Segmentation*, edited by Richard Edwards et al. Lexington, MA: DC Heath.

Piore, M. J. 1979. *Birds of Passage: Migrant Labor and Industrial Societies*. Cambridge: Cambridge University Press.

Polachek, Solomon W. and Francis W. Horvath. 1977. "A Life Cycle Approach to Migration: Analysis of the Perspicacious Peregrinator." *Research in Labor Economics* 1:103-149.

Portes, Alejandro and Robert L. Bach. 1980. "Immigrant Earnings: Cuban and Mexican Immigrants in the United States." *International Migration Review* 14(3):315-341.

Portes, Alejandro. 1984. "The Rise of Ethnicity: Determinants of Ethnic Perceptions Among Cuban Exiles in Miami." *American Sociological Review* 49:383-397

President's Commission on Immigration and Naturalization. 1953. *Whom Shall We Welcome?* Washington, DC: Government Printing Office.

221

Rayback, Joseph G. 1966. *A History of American Labor*. New York: Free Press.

Reder, Melvin W. 1963. "The Economic Consequences of Increased Immigration." *Review of Economics and Statistics* 45(3): 221-230.

Rexroat, Cynthia, and C. Shehan. 1984. "Expected Versus Actual Work Roles of Women." *American Sociological Review* 49:349-358.

Ritchey, P. N. 1976. "Explanations of Migration." *Annual Review of Sociology* 2:363-404.

Rosberg, Gerald M. 1978. "Legal Regulation of the Migration Process: The 'Crisis' of Illegal Immigration." Pp. 336-376 in *Human Migration*, edited by W. H. McNeil and R. S. Adams. Bloomington: Indiana University Press.

Rosenzweig, M. R. 1976. "Nonlinear Earnings Functions, Age, and Experience: A Non Dogmatic Reply and Some Additional Evidence." *Journal of Human Resources* 11:8-22.

Schultz, T. W. 1961. "Investment in Human Capital." *American Economic Review* 2:1-17.

Shaw, P. 1975. Migration Theory and Fact: *A Review and Bibliography of Current Literature*. Philadelphia: Regional Science Research Center.

Simon, Julian L. 1984. "Immigrants, Taxes, and Welfare in the United States." *Population and Development Review* 10(1):53-69.

Simon, Julian L. and Stephen Moore. 1984. "The Effect of Immigration Upon Unemployment." Unpublished Manuscript.

Sjaastad, L. A. 1962. "The Costs and Returns of Human Migration." *Journal of Political Economy* 7:80-93.

Smith, B. and R. Newman. 1977. "Depressed Wages Along the U.S.-Mexican Border: An Empirical Analysis." *Economic Inquiry* 15(1):51-66.

Spengler, J. J. and G. Myers. 1977. "Migration and Socioeconomic Development: Today and Yesterday." Pp. 11-35 in *International Migration: A Comparative Perspective*, edited by A. Brown and E. Neuberger. New York: Academic Press.

Stevens, Gillian, and Joo Hyun Cho. 1985. "Socioeconomic Indexes and the New 1980 Census Occupational Classification Scheme." *Social Science Research* 14:142-168.

Stolzenberg, R. M. 1975a. "Occupations, Labor Markets and the Process of Wage Attainment." *American Sociological Review* 40(5):645-665.

Stolzenberg, R. 1975b. "Education, Occupation, and Wage Differences Between White and Black Men." *American Journal of Sociology* 81:299-324.

Sullivan, Teresa A. 1984. "The Occupational Prestige of Women Immigrants: A Comparison of Cubans and Mexicans." *International Migration Review* 18(4):1045-1062.

Tanton, John and Wayne Lutton. 1993. "Immigration and Criminality in the U.S.A." *Journal of Social, Political and Economic Studies* 18:217-234.

Taylor, Philip. 1971. *The Distant Magnet*. London: Eyre and Spottiswoode.

Temme, L. 1975. *Occupation: Meanings and Measures*. Washington, DC: Bureau of Social Science Research.

Tienda, Marta. 1983. "Market Characteristics and Hispanic Earnings: A Comparison of Natives and Hispanics." *Social Problems* 31(1):59-72.

Tienda, Marta, Leif Jensen, and Robert L. Bach. 1984. "Immigration, Gender and the Process of Occupational Change in the United States, 1970-80." *International Migration Review* 18(4):1021-1044.

Tienda, Marta and Leif Jensen. 1986. "Immigration and Public Assistance Participation: Dispelling the Myth of Dependency." *Social Science Research* 15:372-400.

Todaro, Michael P. and Lydia Maruszko. 1987. Illegal Migration and U.S. Immigration Reform: A Conceptual Framework." *Population and Development Review* 13(1):101-114.

Tolbert, Charles, P. M. Horan, and E. M. Beck. 1980. "The Structure of Economic Segmentation: A Dual Economy Approach." *American Journal of Sociology* 85(5):1095-1116.

Treiman, D. J. 1977. *Occupational Prestige in Comparative Perspective*. New York: Academic Press.

Unz, Ron K. 1994. "Immigration or the Welfare State: Which is our Real Enemy?" *Policy Review* Fall:33-38.

U.S. Bureau of the Census. 1990. *Migration Between the United States and Canada.* Current Population Reports, Series P-23, No. 161. Washington, DC: Government Printing Office.

U.S. Bureau of the Census. 1983a. *Census of Population and Housing, 1980:Public-Use Microdata Samples Technical Documentation.* Prepared by the Data User Services Division, Bureau of the Census. Washington, DC: Government Printing Office.

U.S. Commission on Civil Rights. 1978. *Social Indicators of Equality for Minorities and Women.* Washington, D.C. the Commission.

U.S. Congress Senate Committee on the Judiciary. 1950. *The Immigration and Naturalization Systems of the United States.* Washington, DC: Government Printing Office.

U.S. Congress Senate Committee on the Judiciary. 1979. *Immigration Law and Policy, 1952-1979.* Washington, DC: Government Printing Office.

U.S. Congress. 1986. *Immigration Reform and Control Act of 1986.* PL 99-603, S.1200, November 6. Washington, DC: Government Printing Office.

U.S. Department of Justice, Immigration and Naturalization Service. 1982. *1979 Statistical Yearbook of the Immigration and Naturalization Service.* Washington, DC: Government Printing Office.

U.S. Department of Justice, Immigration and Naturalization Service. 1986. *1984 Statistical Yearbook of the Immigration and Naturalization Service.* Washington, DC: Government Printing Office (Table 1.2).

U.S. Department of Justice, Immigration and Naturalization Service. 1993. *Statistical Yearbook of the Immigration and Naturalization Service, 1992.* Washington, DC: Government Printing Office, Pp. 27-28.

Van Arsdol, Maurice D., Joan, W., David Heer, and Susan Paulvier Haynie. 1979. *Non-Apprehended and Apprehended Undocumented Residents in the Los Angeles Labor Markets: An Exploratory Study.* University of Southern California: Population Research Laboratory.

224

Vasquez, Mario. 1981. "Immigrant Workers in the Apparel Industry in Southern California." In *Mexican Immigrant Workers in the U.S.*, edited by A. Rios-Bustamente. Chicano Research Studies Center, Anthology No. 2, University of California at Los Angeles.

Wachtel, H. M. 1972. "Capitalism and Poverty in America: Paradox or Contradiction?" *American Economic Review* 62:187-194.

Wachter, Michael L. 1980. "The Labor Market and Illegal Immigration: The Outlook for the 1980s." *Industrial and Labor Relations Review* 33(3):342-354.

Waldinger, Roger. 1983. *Ethnic Enterprise and Industrial Change: A Case Study of the New York Garment Industry.* Ph.D. dissertation, Harvard University.

Wallace, Michael and A. L. Kalleberg. 1981. "Economic Organization of Firms and Labor Market Consequences: Toward a Specification of Dual Economy Theory." Pp. 77-117 in *Sociological Perspectives on Labor Markets*, edited by Ivar Berg. New York: Academic Press.

Weintraub, Sidney. 1984. "Illegal Immigrants in Texas: Impact on Social Services and Related Considerations." *International Migration Review* 18(3):733-747.

Wilson, K. L. 1978. "Toward an Improved Explanation of Income Attainment: Re-Calibrating Education and Occupation." *American Journal of Sociology* 84:684-697.

Winner, Irene P. and Rudolph M. Susel. 1983. *The Dynamics of East European Ethnicity Outside of Eastern Europe: With Special Emphasis on the American Case.* Cambridge, MA: Schenkman Publishing Company.

Wise, Donald E. 1974. "The Effect of the Bracero on Agricultural Production in California." *Economic Inquiry* 12(4):267-277.

Wood, Charles H. 1982. "Equilibrium and Historical-Structural Perspectives on Migration." *International Migration Review* 16(2):298-319.

Zucker, Lynne G. and C. Rosenstein. 1981. "Taxonomies of Institutional Structure: Dual Economy Reconsidered." *American Sociological Review* 46:869-884.

Index

227

INDEX